BACKROADS

—— *of* ——

WASHINGTON

BACKROADS

—— of ——

WASHINGTON

Your Guide to Washington's Most Scenic Backroad Adventures

TEXT BY DIANA FAIRBANKS
PHOTOGRAPHY BY MIKE SEDAM

Voyageur Press

Discovery A Pictorial Guide

DEDICATION

To my siblings and my parents, who believed that the best way to learn about
Washington State was to get out and see it.—DF

Dedicated to my sister Carol. May she win her battle.—MS

Edited by Danielle J. Ibister
Designed by Andrea Rud
Maps designed by Maria Friedrich
Printed in China

04   05   06   07   08   5   4   3   2   1

Library of Congress Cataloging-in-Publication Data

Fairbanks, Diana, 1946-
  Backroads of Washington : your guide to Washington's most scenic backroad adventures / text by Diana Fairbanks ; photography by Mike Sedam.
      p. cm. — (A pictorial discovery guide)
  Includes bibliographical references and index.
  ISBN 0-89658-643-X (pbk. : alk. paper)
  1. Automobile travel—Washington (State) 2. Scenic byways—Washington (State)—Guidebooks. 3. Washington (State)—Guidebooks. 4. Washington (State)—Pictorial works. I. Title. II. Series.
  F889.3.F35 2004
  917.9704′44—dc22
                          2004012604

Published by Voyageur Press, Inc.
123 North Second Street, P.O. Box 338, Stillwater, MN 55082 U.S.A.
651-430-2210, fax 651-430-2211
books@voyageurpress.com
www.voyageurpress.com

Educators, fundraisers, premium and gift buyers, publicists, and marketing managers: Looking for creative products and new sales ideas? Voyageur Press books are available at special discounts when purchased in quantities, and special editions can be created to your specifications. For details contact the marketing department at 800-888-9653.

TITLE PAGE:
Summer fog fills the valleys below the road to spectacular Hurricane Ridge.

TITLE PAGE, INSET:
Wild foxglove (Digitalis purpurea) *grows in abundance on the Olympic Peninsula.*

CONTENTS

INTRODUCTION

Hurricane Ridge Visitor's Center offers this view of Elwah Canyon looking up toward Mount Scott and Mount Ferry. The dominant species—Sitka spruce, Douglas fir and western hemlock—can grow to tremendous size, reaching up to three hundred feet in height and twenty-three feet in circumference.

Tasty Red Delicious apples, harvested in the fall, will be packed into controlled-atmosphere storage to await shipment to please palates around the globe.

Photographer Mike Sedam and I both remember the now-extinct Sunday Drive. We have compared notes and found that neither of us is sure what this childhood ritual was intended to accomplish or even how it got started, but sometimes it was a weekly event. Each of us remember Mom and Dad piling the kids in the car along with a picnic cooler and a road map. The adventure always began with a stop at the gas station for fuel, clean windows, and a bottle of soda.

Summer vacations and long weekends expanded on this basic idea with more aimless driving and stops at parks, scenic attractions, and favorite activities. In the process, kids "disagreed," bonded, played games, sang until driver distraction, and learned much about the history of our magical place. Each of us became citizens of our State of Washington by seeing much of it from an open car window and traveling the black-top ribbons that wind through it. I kept a map record and diary of places my family visited on these trips; Mike returned to his favorite places with his first car as a teenager.

It should be no surprise that Mike and I each have our personal favorite highways into the heart of our state. We do agree that the beaches of the West Coast and the Olympic Peninsula are secret pleasures, best enjoyed on a summer afternoon when you tell no one where you are going.

I fondly recall family drives over the Cascade Mountains to visit grandparents in eastern Washington. We took one of two mountain pass routes. The return drive featured a packet of Grandma's homemade cookies "to be opened at the TOP of the pass" while enjoying spectacular scenery. I have returned to eastern Washington regularly as an adult to study and teach; getting there continues to be half the fun.

Mike frequently prowls the eastern side of the state for remnants of ghost towns preserved by the dry heat and cold of the Cascade Mountains rain shadow. These areas provide subjects for his fine art photography and feed his passion for local history. He is also an expert on the scenic features of the Columbia Gorge, which forms the southern boundary between Washington State and Oregon.

Mike and I advocate "poking around" as a travel method. This means you should treat the routes set out here as basic plans begging for embellishment. Carrying bicycles, canoes, cross-country skis, hiking gear, sketchbooks, and cameras is definitely recommended. So is using them. Rubbernecking and frequent stops to gawk are excellent. Picnic coolers and homemade cookies are still appropriate. A tank full of gas is your ticket to adventure; this book is meant to whet your appetite and lead to a renewed appreciation for the lost art of the Sunday Drive.

Be sure to consult a current road map or GPS system for up-to-date highway information, especially in winter and during road construction phases. You won't need an SUV to take these backroads, but a little advance research will reduce surprises. Go on the Internet to learn about amenities and services in the small towns you pass through; almost every small town has a website set up for that purpose. Services may range from resorts and department stores to small convenience stores with no comfort facilities. Gasoline can be precious on some of these routes. Web sites maintained by government agencies will tell you about features, regulations, and accommodations at parks, refuges, recreation sites, and wilderness areas. These resources would have been bliss for planning our childhood Sunday Drives; take advantage of them now. Or you can head out, as our parents did in an earlier time, with a car full of kids, a tank of gas, enough cash for hamburgers, and pure curiosity.

However you proceed, the word from here is "go." Washington State is a magnificent playground scattered with spectacular backroads. A sense of adventure is required. A lifetime of memories is included free.

WASHINGTON

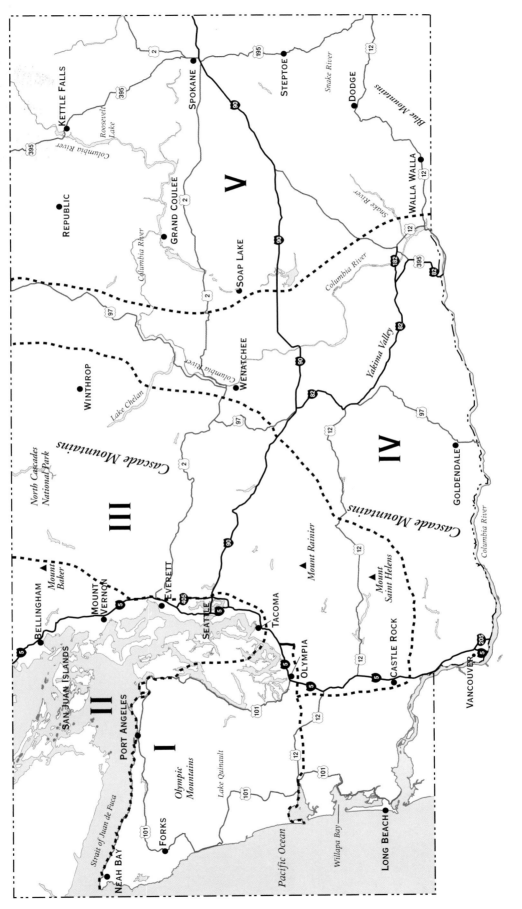

Numbers I–V indicate the regions covered in each section of the book

PART I

OLYMPIC
PENINSULA

FACING PAGE:

The temperate rain forest is a realm where mosses and ferns cling to overhead branches and seedlings carpet downed nurse logs. Minute soil fungi play a part in nourishing conifer trees that tower 150 to 200 feet overhead. Elk and deer browse and trample brush and small trees, allowing more sunlight into the forest.

ABOVE:

Razor clam digging, on Pacific Ocean beaches, is sandy, wet work. Diggers use a tube or a special shovel called a clam gun.

In the modern era, cities and towns built on the wealth of timber harvest and seaport trade still show the rough and sturdy character of their origins. They stand with little alteration because time has largely forgotten them. The beneficiaries are day-trippers who enjoy historic architecture, a quiet small-town pace, and a new emphasis on the arts as an economic force.

But all these charms are merely diversions from the geology and nature of the Olympic Peninsula. Here is the heart of the matter. This unique piece of land represents the collision of two continental plates, with the Olympic Mountain Range marking the crush. The peninsula receives constant washes of moist current on the Pacific Jet Stream, direct from tropical origins, and hosts one of the largest temperate rain forests on the planet. The Olympic Peninsula has withstood glacial carving from numerous ice ages and served as an island for species of plants and animals that now exist nowhere else. Its forested slopes and broad bays drain some of the continent's most beautiful and productive rivers; its high mountain lakes are still pristine and breathtaking. People have built their roads and towns all around the mountains of the peninsula and stayed there, despite economic challenges, because the natural beauty of their region is an everyday fact of life. And residents of Seattle and other large cities nearby and across the country have escaped to the peninsula to recalibrate their pace and taste a simpler and richer encounter with nature.

So you have been warned. The Olympic Peninsula backroads selected here are just a small sample of the possibilities. Feel free to take appealing side roads; you will surely be rewarded for your choices. Get out of your car (nobody has yet melted in the rain here) and smell the forests and ocean beaches. Attend a play or concert at an arts festival. Eat fresh-caught seafood served with refreshing hospitality at a roadside café. Toss the tent in the trunk of your car and fall asleep to the pounding of the surf or the gurgling of a brook. Take the kids fishing at one of the many lakes. If you are on a tight schedule, or just timid, a drive-by shooting with your camera may be just enough to jolt you out of your routine. The Olympic Peninsula does that to visitors.

STRAIT OF JUAN DE FUCA
Sequim to Neah Bay

Ice age glaciers carved a fjord that became a boundary between two countries. While it separates nations and cultures, the Strait of Juan de Fuca also provides a channel to inland harbors for Pacific Ocean weather and ocean life. Early peoples living on either side of the strait specialized in building and powering canoes designed to take advantage of wind and currents. They used them to fish, hunt whales and seals, visit kinsmen, and make war; they also traded these excellent boats to other coastal groups.

This route traces the entire northern edge of the Olympic Peninsula

ROUTE 1

From Sequim Bay State Park just east of Sequim, follow U.S. Highway 101 West to Port Angeles. Continue west four more miles and turn right onto Washington Highway 112. In Pysht, at the junction with Washington Highway 113, turn right to stay on Highway 112 to Clallam Bay and Sekiu. Two miles beyond Sekiu, either turn left on Hoko-Ozette Road or stay on Highway 112 to go to Neah Bay. Turn left in Neah Bay for a road to Cape Flattery.

FACING PAGE:

Hikers enjoy the spectacular view of Sol Duc Falls. This trail takes visitors on an easy 0.9-mile stroll through old growth forest typical of the beauty of western temperate rainforests.

LEFT:

The fish processing boat Red Baron *lays at rest in Port Angeles Harbor.*

ABOVE:

Tatoosh Island, the most northwesterly point in the continental United States, is located a few short miles from Neah Bay on the Makah Indian Reservation. The red-roofed building is the Cape Flattery Lighthouse, built in 1857.

from Sequim to Neah Bay on the Makah Indian Reservation. It takes travelers from modern seaports to archeological digs with plenty of recreation opportunities in between. The constant presence in this journey is the waters of the Pacific Ocean and the strait.

Sequim Bay State Park offers full camping services. Travelers who boat this byway find harbor at the John Wayne Marina. Just west of Sequim on U.S. 101, note a right turn to the Dungeness National Wildlife Refuge, the tiny town of Dungeness, and Dungeness Spit, site of birding and hiking areas and the Dungeness Lighthouse.

Travel west on U.S. 101 to Port Angeles. All services and a helpful visitor center are found here. Besides being a gateway to Hurricane Ridge in Olympic National Park, Port Angeles has ferry connections to Vancouver Island and charters for salmon fishing and whale watching. Ediz Hook is another sandspit with birding potential.

Proceed west on U.S. 101 for about four miles and then turn right on Washington Highway 112 to Neah Bay. A bridge shortly after the junction spans the Elwha River's deep canyon in style. Look for signs to the Salt Creek State Park after turning onto Highway 112. Salt Creek is at the start of the Crescent Bay loop. Joyce, west of Port Angeles, is tiny, but has a gas station. The Lyre River State Park exit is west of Joyce.

The Makah tribe of Neah Bay has a history of making and skillfully using seaworthy wooden boats. Photographer Asahel Curtis took this 1910 photo of Lighthouse Joe posing with a splendid example of a whaling boat. (Courtesy of the Washington State Historical Society)

At the Lyre River, the highway curves inland around a knoll and then follows the strait closely. In this stretch to Pillar Point, and again from the Hoko-Ozette Road to Neah Bay, Highway 112 is a fragile road. It's exposed to flooding from creeks and rivers draining from adjacent hills, as well as weather from the strait. From time to time, parts of the road have washed out, so be sure to ask about the road ahead at Port Angeles or Joyce. The trade-off for its vulnerability is that this road has incredible views of shoreline rock formations and the strait and Vancouver Island. There is little traffic to complicate sightseeing.

Pillar Point State Park, near the town of Pysht, celebrates those shoreline rock formations. At Pysht, Highway 112 works inland along the Pysht River to meet Washington Highway 113. Stay on Highway 112 as it turns right, back toward the strait, and meets up with the water again at Clallam Bay. There are two campgrounds and boat launching facilities on the bay. The town of Clallam Bay sits on the east side of the bay and the fishing town of Sekiu sits on the west.

About two miles west of Sekiu, observe a turnoff to Hoko-Ozette Road. Latent archeologists will lobby for a trip to Ozette Lake. The state park there has all amenities and anchors the hike to the Cape Alava archeological site, which has yielded so much about the lifestyle of an ancient Makah village. Ozette Lake has an interpretive center as well.

Travelers who don't "dig" archeology should continue west on Highway 112 to Neah Bay. This section of road again hugs the strait and provides outstanding scenery. Eagles, puffins, auklets, otters, and gray whales live in this habitat. Keep your camera and binoculars handy here. Continuing on, enter the Makah Indian Reservation and the town of Neah Bay. This is the home of ancient and modern fishermen and charter boat captains.

An excellent tribal cultural center in town distills the Ozette Lake site finds. The tribe publicly celebrates its heritage with the annual Makah Days festivities in late summer. Ask for directions to Cape Flattery, the westernmost point in the lower forty-eight states. Tribal lands permit fees may be charged. The road to Cape Flattery winds around the southwest coast to a parking area near Flattery Creek. Take the thirty-minute hike to the overlook at the tip of Cape Flattery, with fabulous views of Tatoosh Island and the Cape Flattery Lighthouse.

The Strait of Juan de Fuca was named for a sixteenth-century Greek explorer, employed by the crown of Spain to search the western coastline of North America for a fabled Straits of Anain. The strait actually received its name two centuries later, in 1788, when Captain John Meares determined that he had re-discovered the waterway described in Juan de Fuca's records.

Olympic Mountains
Port Angeles to Hurricane Ridge

ROUTE 2

From the Olympic National Park Visitor Center just outside Port Angeles, head south about twenty miles to Hurricane Ridge, where the road terminates just beyond the Hurricane Ridge Visitor Center.

Residents of Seattle can see mountains on every side: Mount Rainier dominates the south view, the Cascades are to the east, and Mount Baker is a distant sentinel to the north. After looking at the Olympics in toothed sunsets, many want to travel there. The long way to tour is to take a weekend and drive a loop around the Olympic Peninsula. The short way is to drive this route. Its total length is twenty miles from Port Angeles to the end of the road at Hurricane Ridge.

Port Angeles is a modern shipping terminal handling timber, petroleum, ocean products, and other goods of trade partners on the Pacific Ocean. All services are available here, including rentals and guide services for wilderness recreation. You can also book whale-watching tours and sports-fishing charters. The south end of Vancouver Island, Canada, is visible across the Strait of Juan de Fuca from the Port Angeles waterfront. A ferry to the island departs from Port Angeles Harbor. The town is backed up against the Olympic Mountains, with foothills rising to glaciered peaks that are nearly a mile high.

The peninsula and the mountains are relatively late additions to the North American continent, if twelve million years can be called recent. They are the remains of the old continental plate edge that pushed toward the larger continental mass while new plate edges were evolving. Some areas of the mountains show their origins as volcanic formations that can only be created beneath the sea; the folded layers of sedimentary rock in the Olympics set them apart from the volcanic mountains of the Cascade

Many spots in Hurricane Ridge appear to have suffered a small burn or forest fire. Most, like the one pictured here, were damaged by high winds, which are common in winter months. That's why they call it Hurricane Ridge.

Late snow caps the peaks of the Bailey Range in early summer. The snow is usually gone by the fourth of July. Drivers can access the road to Hurricane Ridge all year long (with occasional weather exceptions).

The mountain goat (Oreamnos americanus) was introduced to Olympic National Forest in the 1920s. Goats are occasionally seen in the highcountry of the park lands.

Piper's bellflower (Campanula piperi) is one of the rare wild flowers unique to the Olympics. In July and August, the upper elevations flourish with reds, yellows, and pinks from great fields of mixed wild-flower blooms.

Mountains. On Hurricane Ridge, these traits are on dramatic display at high altitude, capped by active glaciers.

From downtown Port Angeles, drive south toward the park; the route is well marked from U.S. 101. Just a mile from the highway is the national park's visitor center. The road from here to Heart O' the Hills campground lies within the park's boundary. Be sure to choose the right fork when the road splits just a ways past the visitor center. The road rises over a row of foothills then burrows into deep-forested mountainside. The north end of the Klahhane Range forces the road to turn east and climb around Burnt Mountain. Then it clings to the ridge high above the Morse Creek drainage as it climbs to Hurricane Ridge. This plan yields some pullouts with spectacular views. At ten miles outside of Port Angeles, there is a viewpoint that reveals an excellent vista, in clear weather, of the Dungeness Spit east of the town. Another turnoff opportunity is at thirteen miles.

Besides the vistas, this backroad has pristine mountain forests and the occasional Columbia black-tailed deer. A pullout at sixteen miles serves as a trailhead for hikers using the Switchback Trail up Klahhane Ridge. Now the road rises into alpine territory with meadows that bloom luxuriantly just after snowmelt.

Arrive at the visitor center at Hurricane Ridge. The lodge offers food service, sightseeing information, and an interpretive center. On a clear warm afternoon, visitors from all over the world wander the alpine trails and take zillions of pictures. Very few places offer such spectacular views to motorists. Hikers count it as a jumping-off place for trails that travel deep into the heart of the Olympic Range. Rangers guide short foot-tours to introduce the unique ecological features of the park and the mountain range. The road is open year-round, and the park offers skiing and snowshoeing in winter.

Countless artists have captured Hurricane Ridge in paintings and photography; consider bringing such tools if the weather promises to cooperate. It would be a shame to visit this beautiful place without taking a little of it back to nourish the soul later.

HOOD CANAL
Quilcene to Shelton

ROUTE 3

From Quilcene, follow U.S. Highway 101 South through the towns of Brinnon, Eldon, Lilliwaup, Hoodsport, and Potlatch, ending at Shelton.

Words that describe this backroad: winding, slithering, undulating, twisting, rolling, snaking, meandering, hillside-hugging, squiggly, and charming. U.S. 101 follows the rain shadow side of the Olympic Mountains as they plunge into Hood Canal. This fjord divides the Kitsap from the Olympic Peninsula. It provides a record of an ancient collision of continents and subsequent ice ages that affected the current contours of Puget Sound. The fertile blue waters are bounded by the green-forested arms of the Olympic National Forest and tall, iced mountains. No wonder the shoreline and towns on this byway are dotted with summer homes and parks: Hood Canal is the perfect summertime getaway.

In 1913, photographer Edward S. Curtis captured this elegant image of a Skokomish chief's daughter. Documenting a vanishing way of life, Curtis—the estranged brother of celebrated Pacific Northwest photographer Asahel Curtis—spent over thirty years producing a definitive collection of images of Native Americans from eighty different tribes.

Quilcene is the name given to both the town at the beginning of the route and the native oysters of this region. The town's seafood restaurants specialize in—what else?—oysters. A short drive on Linger Longer Road (turn off U.S. 101 at the Whistling Oyster restaurant) ends at Dabob Bay, which features a public boat launch and an oyster hatchery. The bay is as easy to reach by boat as it is by car.

Heading south on U.S. 101, stop at the Quilcene Ranger Station. Olympic National Forest information, maps, books, permits, and natural history information are dispensed here. Learn about salmon species indigenous to this area, and see them begin their odyssey at the nearby Quilcene fish hatchery. Then embark on the work of enjoying fabulous views and deciding among forest recreation options.

The first stopover to consider is Falls View Campground (a left turn) or Mount Walker Viewpoint (a right turn). If time is short, choose Mount Walker. Drive to the top of the mountain among banks of native rhododendrons in spring, and arrive at spectacular vistas any time of year.

High mountain runoff flows swiftly over rocks in the Duckabush River.

Located in the town of Union on the lower Hood Canal, the Dalby Water Wheel operated as one of the first hydroelectric plants in western Washington.

LEFT:

Rhododendrons are the Washington state flower. Just come to Mount Walker, less than ten miles from Quilcene, in May. You can't miss 'em.

BELOW:

Rhododendron (Rhododendron macrophyllum) means "rose tree with large leaves."

Other parks and stopping places tempt the traveler on the drive between Quilcene and Brinnon, including Seal Rocks and Dosewallips estuary, which nurtures wetland wildlife. Gardeners and rhododendron fans should schedule a stop at Whitney Gardens and Nursery. "Rhodies" are Washington's state flower and their varieties are exuberant; most are represented here.

Brinnon offers marinas, charters, seafood, and a turnoff to the Brothers Wilderness area. South of town is tiny Quatsap Point with Pleasant Harbor State Park on its north margin and the Duckabush estuary on the south. At Duckabush, an access road leads to more recreation sites in the Brothers Wilderness area. Triton Cove offers waterfront picnic sites. Two miles north of Eldon, a turnoff at the Hamma Hamma River gives access to Lena Lake and Hamma Hamma Recreation Areas.

Between Eldon and Lilliwaup are even more reasons to keep a tent and hiking boots in the trunk of the car. Eagle Creek and Melbourne Lake campsites are good examples. Or stop off at Tidelands State Park adjacent to the town of Lilliwaup.

In the town of Hoodsport, exit at Washington Highway 119 to access the Olympic National Park. That road also takes you past Staircase, Lake Cushman, and Hoodsport Trail State Parks.

South of Hoodsport on U.S. 101, the town of Potlatch marks the northern boundary of the Skokomish Indian Reservation. It's only two more miles to the town of Skokomish but another park, Potlatch State Park, is found in that interval. At Skokomish, contemplate a side trip to the "summer home" town of Union, east on Washington Highway 3. This road swings around the south end of Hood Canal through the Skokomish Valley and brings travelers to face the exquisite Olympic Mountains towering over the banks of the canal. Twanoh (another name for Skokomish) State Park is on this road.

Back on U.S. 101, it is just under ten miles through the valley from Skokomish to Shelton. The latter town serves as a re-entry point into civilization, or a place to stock and re-stock for summer fun. This city on Oakland Bay has an annual Oysterfest in October, featuring mass consumption of the tasty bivalves. The town's historical museum provides the story of early timber days. You provide your own history of fun and recreation on the Hood Canal backroads.

If you need to return to the larger metropolitan cities on Puget Sound, turn north on Highway 3 to Bremerton, which provides ferries across the sound. Or drive south to Olympia at the southern end of the sound and then north on Interstate 5.

RAIN FOREST
La Push to Lake Quinault

ROUTE 4

The term "rain forest" conjures an image of thick, steamy jungles alive with plants and exotic animals. This byway relishes an even more exclusive environment, a temperate rain forest. It's like a tropical rain forest, only cooler.

Begin at the beach town of La Push, where a ranger station supplies maps and information about Olympic National Forest and Olympic National Park. This byway, from La Push to Queets, lies within the Olympic National Forest.

Drive east on Highway 110 to connect with U.S. 101 at Forks. The nearby forks of the Bogachiel, Calawah, and Sol Duc Rivers suggest its name. This town has a history with its forests and a Timber Museum to explain it. Logging has always been the principal industry in this area.

From La Push, travel east on Washington Highway 110 toward Forks. There, turn right on U.S. Highway 101 and follow it south. Turn off east at one or more rain forest sites within the Olympic National Forest and National Park. Back on U.S. 101, drive south to Queets, then follow the highway southeast toward Quinault. End with a circle of Lake Quinault.

Logging old-growth wood was one of Washington's first industries. Loggers cut this specimen around 1940 when trucks and motorized hoists were available to assist with the rugged, dangerous work.

A stream meanders through the Quinault watershed. Because of year-round rain, these streams never run dry, making them fertile places for many unique types of aquatic life.

Roosevelt elk frequent rain forest valleys in the winter and early spring. During summer, they move up the mountain slopes to higher elevations.

Heavy moss clings to a limb in the Hoh Rain Forest. Moisture-laden clouds pushed in from the Pacific Ocean supply the rain needed to nourish this amazing ecosystem.

A palette of green dominates the Hall of Mosses Trail in the Hoh Rain Forest of Olympic National Park. The park boundaries include exceptional wilderness beaches and rugged snow-covered peaks. The most spectacular assets, however, are the rain forests, home to a magnificent collection of giant conifers. Some are the largest of their type in the world.

Logging equipment, information on logging methods, and re-created living spaces in the museum show the loggers' life in the early days and trace the changes in the technology and ecology of harvesting timberlands. The museum also includes information on railroad lines. Services are available in Forks; this is the last chance to pick up a raincoat. There is a Forest Service/National Park Service information station at Forks where intrepid hikers get their permits.

Now drive south on U.S. 101 to the first of several places to encounter the temperate rain forest: the Bogachiel State Park and campground, which invites stopping, tenting, hiking, and gawking at the huge old trees amid exorbitant stands of green. This is the starting place for treks into the Olympic Mountains along the Bogachiel River Valley.

U.S. 101 continues south into the Hoh River Valley and to the turnoff to the most popular rain forest experience. This stretch of highway features tree farms and forests. Almost ten miles from the park is the turnoff to the Hoh Rain Forest Visitor Center, deep in the valley carved by this

A Washington Sapling. Copyrighted by Frank Palmer.

The first logging operations involved cutting giant trees by hand. The work was grueling and hazardous. These 1909 loggers show the scale of their task.

fertile river. The Hoh Rain Forest Visitor Center is less than twenty miles from U.S. 101. The road to the visitor center passes the Willoughby Creek and Minnie Peterson campgrounds to arrive at an even larger recreation site, which is complete with information materials and helpful personnel, as well as picnic grounds, campsites, and trailheads into the Olympic Mountains. Trails through the forest have helpful signage. Permits for backcountry expeditions and rafting are available here. Roosevelt elk make stately parades through the park meadows.

The English language has surprisingly limited vocabulary to describe greenness. It all gets puts to work here. The soft forest floor, the tall pillar-like trees, and the green canopy make the forest feel like a cathedral. Sound behaves differently here, echoing softly and muffled by millions of fronds, leaves, needles, and mosses. All of this is a temple that water built. Streams, falls, and raindrops are the music.

Returning to U.S. 101, drive south again and note more camping facilities available on the river at Cottonwood and Hoh Oxbow campgrounds. The next stop is Kalaloch. This town has gas and services, a campground, and the Kalaloch Information Station. The South Beach campground, a couple of miles south of town, sits just at the edge of the Quinault Indian Reservation. A short distance from the campground, on the reservation, is the town of Queets; almost five miles beyond that is a turnoff to the Copper Mine Bottom, Upper Clearwater, and Yahoo Lake campgrounds on the Clearwater River. Beyond that second turnoff is another, which leads to the Queets River campground. This detour into the woods features the largest Douglas fir in the Olympic National Park, visible after a four-mile hike from the campground. Feel dwarfed.

From the Queets River turnoff, follow U.S. 101 to the North Shore Road exit at Lake Quinault. This begins a route around the lake and along two forks of the Quinault River above it; this drive offers seven campgrounds, four ranger stations, three interpretive trails, and two boat launches.

Only a mile after leaving U.S. 101, signs indicate a short hike to the national park's largest western red cedar. The valley cradling Lake Quinault and the Quinault River is home to hundreds of deer and elk, which stalk majestically through lowland grasslands, munching, munching, munching! Hikers drive to Graves Creek and begin treks into Enchanted Valley and to the Dosewallips River on the west side of Olympic National Park. The fishing in all the waterways here is excellent. Quiet, cool campgrounds are tempting, popular escapes on hot summer weekends.

The Quinault, Queets, and Hoh river valleys enjoy protection under the auspices of the national park, and include some of the most magnificent examples of temperate rain forest ecosystem and Sitka spruce stands in the world. Any rain forest, tropical or temperate, features rain, and the western slopes of the Olympic Range get twelve to fourteen feet of it

ABOVE:

This view down the beach, of Split Rock, is typical of the rock formations and beach access parks west of Forks on Washington Highway 110.

RIGHT:

Surf-tumbled beach rocks glisten after a fresh wave. Many ocean beaches on the peninsula are sand flats, but a couple of them are noted for rounded beach rocks.

Colorful floats, formerly used to mark crab pots, now decorate a fence near Hoquiam.

Commercial fishing boats moor in front of a dry dock in a river near Hoquiam.

every year. Temperature is the condition that sets temperate rain forests apart; average temperatures in these valleys range from freezing to 80 degrees Fahrenheit. As in tropical forests, every conceivable inch of the environment is filled with plants and the animals that depend on them. The temperate rain forest in the Olympic National Park and National Forest is a treasure, because it is more rare than tropical rain forests, easily accessible for visitors from the Puget Sound metropolis, and a world away from suburban life.

WILD BEACHES
La Push to Hoquiam via U.S. Highway 101

ROUTE 5

From La Push, travel east on Washington Highway 110 toward Forks. There, turn right on U.S. Highway 101 and follow it south to Queets, then follow the highway southeast toward Lake Quinault. At the south end of the lake, follow U.S. 101 South to Hoquiam and Aberdeen.

Technically, this backroad route follows much of the same rain forest route detailed in the previous backroad. That byway featured the interior rain forest flanking the east side of the highway. This time around, the emphasis is on the wondrous coastal beaches on the west side of U.S. 101.

Geologically, the Olympic Peninsula is merely twelve million years or so old, making it a relatively late add-on to the continent of North America. Those who travel this byway glory in the annex and all its features. Rain forests, mountains, fertile rivers, timber, beaches, and quiet trails are all available to adventurers.

The start of this byway is La Push, a small oceanfront town that has been occupied by the Quillayute tribe. Try to visit both sides of the Quillayute River. The La Push Road (Highway 110) goes to First Beach, Second Beach, and Third Beach on the south side of the river. Turn onto Mora Road to get to Rialto Beach. Anticipate some short hikes at the end of the road to reach the waterline; these are well worth the trouble. Bring a picnic and a camera.

In Forks, head south on U.S. 101. The highway eventually turns toward the coast, following the Hoh River to the sea. It pops out of the forest and follows the Pacific Ocean at Ruby Beach and the Hoh Indian Reservation.

This roadway from Ruby Beach to the town of Queets is a summer treat and a winter storm watcher's secret. The road twists and turns, encountering cliffs and deep forests and surprising ocean views. Beaches 6, 5, 4, 3, 2, 1, South Beach, and the Kalaloch Rocks stop cars, especially on the rare clear, warm summer day. Most involve parking the car and hiking through coastal forests to the beach below. Drop by Kalaloch for its information station. Compared to the mountain rain forest, coastal beach forests are dense but neatly clipped by wind and driven rain.

The Quinault Indian Reservation at Queets marks a turn away from the coast for U.S. 101. It follows the Salmon River Valley to beautiful Lake Quinault. The lake, which can be circuited by North and South Shore Roads, has two ranger stations and another rain forest access on its north

Pacific Ocean - Copalis Beach Wash
Ellis 5350

side. July Falls Creek State Parks offer camping and elk. Some services are available at Amanda Park and Quinault. Easy hiking trails surround grand old Lake Quinault Lodge, which proudly serves up fine accommodations for those who don't care to rough it at the beach.

From Quinault, U.S. 101 heads south toward Aberdeen and Hoquiam, the towns that lumber built. Halfway there, you'll arrive at a town whose name causes much merriment: Humptulips. A turnoff takes you to the seaside towns of Pacific Beach, Copalis Beach, and Ocean City.

Hoquiam has a proud logging tradition and many examples of the machines and history that marked its early days. Log shipping and paper-making still generate the dollars here. But its location on Gray's Harbor also makes it the closest large city to the resort area of Ocean Shores and the state park at Ocean City. All kinds of services and supplies are available.

I spent many shining happy moments on these Pacific beaches with my family on summer camping trips. The deep dense forests and wide sand stretches still have a kind of magic. They beg for running with kites, poking in driftwood, looking up at canopies of green, watching animals, getting muddy, cooling off, eating around campfires, and thinking of the world as a big amazing planet. Experience them for yourself and feel like a kid again.

Copalis Beach remains one of the few places where cars may drive on hard-packed beach sand. This auto brought a family in the 1940s right to the surf's edge.

PART II

PUGET SOUND

FACING PAGE:

Mount Baker emerges above its foothills as seen from the fishing village of La Conner, on the west side of the Skagit Valley.

ABOVE:

Seagulls follow Washington State Ferries for curiosity and food handouts from bird-friendly passengers.

Washington's geologic history bestowed on the state advantages that have attracted people, ancient and modern. Puget Sound is one example of those advantages. Formed by a collision of prehistoric continents and gouged by strong arms of ice in glacial periods, this sheltered waterway pushes deep into the state. Its shores bear productive wetlands and practical harbors.

All but one of the major cities in Washington are on Puget Sound. Their economies depend on the clear safe passage to the Pacific Ocean to conduct worldwide trade. Workers harvest food from these waterways and float timber to its collection points. And vacationers launch their boats or board ferries to cross Puget Sound on the way to good times!

Spanish explorers, followed later by English and American explorers, charted the mouth of Puget Sound in their search for the mythical "Inland Passage," a waterway across North America. Their maps and diaries note thriving populations of Native American tribes who fished, hunted, gathered, traded extensively, and developed a complex society and robust art traditions. Explorers also noted prominent coastal landmarks from their ships on the sound.

Westward expansion brought settlers who displaced the tribes as they founded towns and businesses. Decisions about borders with other states and Canada; locations of government offices, cities, roads, and railroads; and the exploitation of peoples and natural resources established many of the traditions that still impact Puget Sound today. For example, Olympia, on the south sound, became the official state capital after much wrangling and speculation among many candidates. Port Townsend, on the Strait of Juan de Fuca, was one of the contenders.

Overhead, Puget Sound provides a protected passage on a major flyway for migrating birds. In the waters below, migrating whales and salmon seek the same advantages. Those who visit the sound experience casual, touching, and amazing encounters with wildlife. Deer swim across tidewaters to island refuges, and sea lions haul out on docks full of vacationers. Volunteers count and observe whale pods, and waterfowl take over busy harbors during their migrations. Eagles roost in trees in city parks, or crowd riverfronts, watching for salmon, while being watched by humans. Communities around Puget Sound take stewardship of their water treasure seriously.

And then there are boats. Puget Sound has more boats per capita than any other area in the nation. Marinas are full, with moorage at a premium. Weekends are for sailboat racing throughout Puget Sound. Car and passenger ferries, and some spectacular bridge engineering, move travelers across the water on "marine highways" managed by Washington's Department of Transportation. Private craft, from kayaks to yachts to fishing boats, dot the water in good weather. Smaller pleasure craft move among freighters, tankers, container ships, submarines, cruise ships, floatplanes, commercial fishing and canning ships, and military vessels using the waters as their highway.

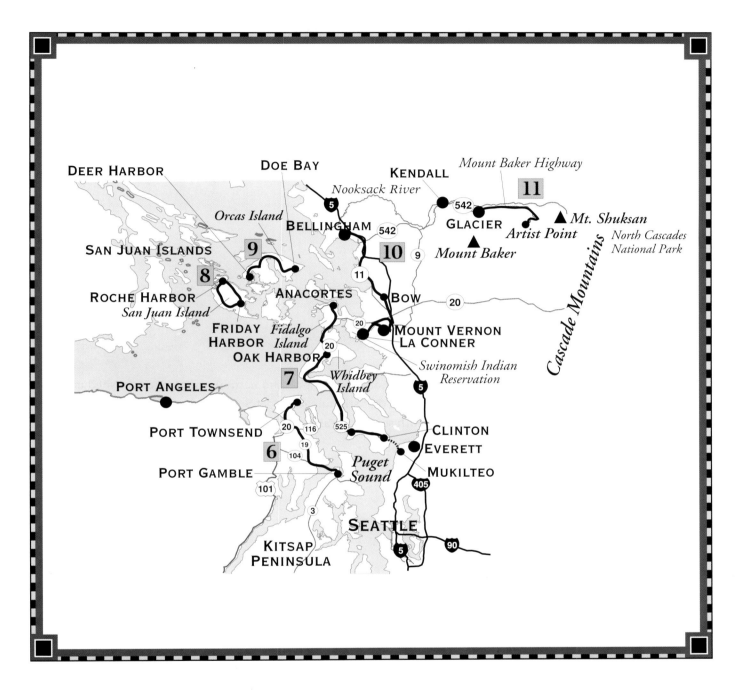

DEER HARBOR

DOE BAY

KENDALL

Mount Baker Highway

11

Nooksack River

5

GLACIER **542**

▲ Mt. Shuksan

Orcas Island

BELLINGHAM **542**

Artist Point

North Cascades National Park

SAN JUAN ISLANDS

9

10 **9**

▲ *Mount Baker*

8

11

Cascade Mountains

ROCHE HARBOR

ANACORTES

BOW

San Juan Island

20

FRIDAY HARBOR *Fidalgo Island*

20

MOUNT VERNON LA CONNER

20

OAK HARBOR

Swinomish Indian Reservation

PORT ANGELES

7

Whidbey Island

5

PORT TOWNSEND

20 **116**

525

CLINTON

6

19

EVERETT

104

Puget Sound

MUKILTEO

PORT GAMBLE

101

405

3

SEATTLE

KITSAP PENINSULA

5

90

LEFT:

The sun sets on the Hood Canal Floating Bridge, casting glowing colors over quiet tidewaters. This vital link between the Kitsap and Olympic Peninsulas carries more than 18,000 cars a day.

ABOVE:

The Washington State Ferry System is the largest in the country and carries over eleven million cars across Puget Sound waters annually.

Some of the byways in this region can be traced by boat or by car, and car ferries do most of the moving on trips to the San Juan Islands. Marine parks—state parks accessible only by boat—can be found throughout Puget Sound.

You'll remember the backroads of Puget Sound for their sunshine. The east side of the waterway lies in the rain shadow of the Olympic Range and experiences drier weather than the west side. Winds from the Pacific Ocean blow strong on the Strait of Juan de Fuca, where bigger ships navigate. The San Juan Islands and north coast experience cold weather patterns that originate in Alaskan and Canadian climes.

The common thread among the Puget Sound byways is the pulse of tides and the weather pushing inland from the great Pacific Ocean. Mount Baker catches more snow than any other place on the continent, due to the merging tropical and arctic weather patterns. This live volcano was first identified from Puget Sound and is the culmination of land's transition from salt water to coastal mountainside. By contrast, the windswept grassy islands of the San Juan group get so little precipitation that they harbor stands of prickly pear cactus.

Get in the car and go see this stuff. Enjoy the fun of being on an island in the sun. Snowboard on a volcano. Drive across tidewaters on a floating bridge. Sit in a vacation harbor with a glass of wine from nearby vineyards. Walk in the places where international history was made. Go fishing. Wind along a rock-walled coastline that even glaciers couldn't compromise. Find artists and crafts workers who draw their inspiration from the beauty of place. Taste seafood, fruit, wines, and cheeses grown and made in the Puget Sound region. But get going quick. Time and tide wait for no one.

THE HISTORY OF PUGET SOUND
Port Gamble to Port Townsend

In 1849, Puget Sound was thick with timber. The S'Klallam peoples had a rich culture in a land abundant with food and shelter. Businessmen originally attracted to the West Coast by the California Gold Rush began to consider Puget Sound's plentiful resources. They saw potential profit in the needs of growing cities of gold seekers. *Teekalet* was the tribal name for the quiet bay that Andrew J. Pope and William C. Talbot considered the perfect site for their new logging mill. Their New England roots were evident in the white clapboard company town they created. Quaint Port Gamble still looks like a misplaced village from Maine.

Start on this historic backroad by touring the town. The Historic Museum and the funky Shell Museum are housed in a large building that also functions as a general store. Other old mill management buildings serve modern village needs. A nearby knoll holds a cemetery with excellent views. The entire town is a National Historic Landmark District; walk

ROUTE 6

The Seattle-Bainbridge or Edmonds-Kingston ferries get Seattleites onto the Kitsap Peninsula to reach Port Gamble at the beginning of this route. A longer trek is south on Interstate 5 to Olympia, then northwest on U.S. Highway 101, and north again at Shelton on Washington Highway 3. West of Port Gamble, follow signs to Washington Highway 104 and the Hood Canal Bridge. Five miles beyond the bridge, turn right on Washington Highway 19. Connect with Washington Highway 20 and follow it to Port Townsend.

around to feel the life of a company worker in the booming lumber industry. The bay beyond the general store still collects logs for shipment, although the nearby mill has been razed.

After your stroll, drive west on Highway 104 towards the Hood Canal Bridge. It is the world's longest concrete floating bridge on tidal waters and gives passage across Hood Canal. As a replacement for a car ferry, it has proven to be the lifeline of all the towns on the northern border of the Olympic Peninsula—so much so that an extra span lies at anchor near Port Gamble in case a storm should take out a section.

Just across the bridge, stop at the beach park to view the structure from sea level. Occasionally, military vessels from nearby Bangor Naval Base, including surfaced submarines, are spotted practicing maneuvers.

Continue west on Highway 104 and turn at the exit for Port Townsend, Port Hadlock, Port Ludlow, and Chimacum. Washington Highway 19 heads north through a beautiful lowland carved by glaciers, streams, and animals. Beaver Valley is a lush green swale created in part by the ambitious rodents. The road then enters the Chimacum Valley, the former home of the Chemakum peoples. The tribe has gone extinct. The broad valley is now occupied by dairy cows and farmers, who live amid sumptuous green pastures that are ringed by deep forests and backed up to the glistening peaks of the Olympic Mountains.

North of Chimacum, a tempting detour looms. A right turn at Washington Highway 116 leads to Port Hadlock (think quintessentially quaint fishing village) and across Indian Island to Marrowstone Island. At the northernmost tip of the latter island is Fort Flagler State Park. This fort and its sister emplacements, Fort Worden and Fort Casey, were built between 1897 and 1911 to guard the approach to the Bremerton Naval Shipyard and the cities of Puget Sound. All three forts now provide beachfront access, museums, and those indestructible concrete bunkers that held the guns of defense.

North of the turnoff to Port Hadlock, Highway 19 connects with Washington Highway 20 from the west near the tiny Jefferson County International Airport. The road climbs a hillside to a crest where travelers overlook the Kah Lagoon. This low wetland seems to form a moat around old Port Townsend, which occupies a headland waterfront, and the hill of pale sand and gravel bluffs above it.

The town looks north to the Strait of Juan de Fuca, east to Whidbey Island, and south into Puget Sound. This location once put it in contention with other growing towns as the government seat for Washington Territory. Port Townsend briefly pulled ahead in this competition by taxing ships heading for trade in the sound. Optimism, busy ports, and timber trade fueled opulent growth and unrestrained Victorian architecture. In the subsequent roller coaster of timber and shipping economies, Port Townsend became a backwater, frozen in its "birthday cake" finery. Now it booms again with tourists and a cadre of artists who live and work here.

ABOVE:
Fishing and pleasure boats idle at Port Hudson just outside the town of Port Townsend.

RIGHT:
Point Wilson signals ships crossing Admiralty Inlet with this lighthouse, surrounded on land by Fort Worden State Park. Across the inlet is Whidbey Island.

Port Gamble, preserved by Pope and Talbot Industries, provides a glimpse into the glory days of timber trade. This church was the pride of the old port.

The Ann Starrett House, built in Port Townsend in 1889, features frescoed ceilings and a freestanding three-story grand staircase.

The waterfront business district offers excellent dining and shopping. On the hill above town, gigantic historic homes with jubilant embellishment have been beautifully restored and given new life.

Port Townsend shares a peninsula with Fort Worden, which reprises the military construction seen at Fort Flagler. Nowadays, the fort's aircraft hangar is more apt to host a concert than a blimp. Art has replaced artillery. Performances and festivals by Centrum, an arts organization, fill the fort's parade grounds with music and color. A marine science museum sits on the pier that tethered surveillance boats.

This byway chronicles the natural and economic history of the Olympic Peninsula, while sampling the pleasures of modern diversions. Enjoy them both.

ISLAND LIFE
Anacortes to Mukilteo

ROUTE 7

To reach Anacortes from Interstate 5, exit on Washington Highway 20 West. When the highway splits into north and south roads, take the north one to Anacortes. From Anacortes, backtrack south on Highway 20 and continue past the Interstate 5 turnoff. Cross over Deception Pass and pass through the towns of Oak Harbor, Coupeville, Greenbank, and Freeland. Continue south on Highway 20, then turn west on Washington Highway 525 toward the town of Clinton, where a ferry ride brings travelers to the mainland at Mukilteo.

The best stories of childhood took place on islands. *Anne of Green Gables*, *Treasure Island*, and *Swiss Family Robinson* fill children's imaginations with high expectations. Fidalgo and Whidbey Islands actually fill the bill for grown-ups, offering stories of history, impressive forts, farms, cozy inns, and adventures on land and sea.

To begin this island trek, reach Anacortes by exiting Interstate 5, heading west on Highway 20. This road crosses the broad flood plain of the Skagit River, passes over the Swinomish Slough, and heads up the rocky hills that comprise Fidalgo Island. Where the highway splits into north and south routes, take the north one to Anacortes. This is a busy and photogenic seaport town where shipping, fishing, pleasure boating, and international travel all compete for harbor space. Stock up for camping, sport fishing, and hiking expeditions here, or book a whale-watching cruise. Car and passenger ferries depart from here for Vancouver Island in Canada.

Backtrack south on Highway 20 and continue past the Interstate 5 turnoff. You'll pass two scenic lakes, Campbell and Pass, and come quickly to Deception Pass. A glorious steel arch bridge spans this magnificent waterway between Fidalgo Island and Whidbey Island. Take a walking tour of the bridge to watch boats navigate the treacherous tides far below. Stop at the surrounding state park, where rocky cliffs, beachside coves, and deep dark forests bring out the pirate games in visitors of all ages. Stay for beautiful sunsets.

Drive twenty miles south on Highway 20—noting an exit to Joseph Whidbey State Park—to the town of Oak Harbor. A large marina awaits boaters, and a municipal park with a startling Dutch windmill lines the shore of this harbor town. The windmill commemorates Oak Harbor's founding in 1894 by a party of immigrants from Holland. All recreation services are available here; this is the largest town on Whidbey Island.

Drawn and Published by E. S. Glover, Portland, Oregon.

Entered according to Act of Congress, in the year 1878, by E. S. Glover, in the Office of the Librarian of Congress, at Washington, D. C.

A. L. Bancroft & Co., Lith., San Francisco, Cal.

BIRD'S EYE VIEW OF
PORT TOWNSEND,
PUGET SOUND, WASHINGTON TERRITORY.

FROM THE NORTH-EAST.

1878.

A—Presbyterian Church.
B—Methodist Church.
C—Episcopal Church.
D—Catholic Church.
E—Cosmopolitan Hotel.

F—Masonic Building.
G—Odd Fellows' Hall.
H—Good Templars' Hall.
I—Red Men's Hall.
J—Public School.

K—Post Office.
L—Court House.
M—Jail Building.
N—Custom House.
O—Dr. Hill's Drug Store.

P—Democratic Press.
Q—Weekly Argus.
R—Rothschild & Co., Shipping Merchants.
S—Fort Townsend.
T—Olimpa Mountains.

Port Townsend's founders had visions of grandeur—and a position to control Puget Sound's boat traffic. This hand-drawn 1878 map suggests the pride taken in the new town's streets and harbors.

FAR LEFT:

Connecting Fidalgo Island to Whidbey Island, the bridge at Deception Pass forms a spectacular arch over swift tidal waters.

LEFT:

A "rumored to be vicious" cat guards a store in the historic town of Coupeville.

BELOW:

The coast guard anchors this cutter at Anacortes, where it has easy access to the Straits of Georgia and Juan de Fuca or Puget Sound.

South again, the highway follows the thin neck of the island through Ebey's Landing National Historic Reserve, a twenty-five-square-mile innovation of public/private land management in National Park Service designations. Within the reserve lies the town of Coupeville. Nearly every enterprise here spotlights the arts. An art center draws teachers and learners from far and wide, and shops showcase the work of artists lucky enough to live in the region. A wooden blockhouse from an early fortification stands just outside of town. Coupeville will remind you of a New England seaside village.

Driving south again within the reserve, visitors have choices to make. Some prefer to hike and bicycle the paths of the low flat area, or pursue kite flying and birding. History buffs visit Fort Ebey, named after the first permanent settler on Whidbey Island, Isaac Ebey. He filed his claim for land in 1850 and lived on the island until 1857, when Haida tribe members beheaded him. The fort, built in 1942, was part of a system guarding the Puget Sound from enemy attack during World War II.

Just around the bend is another behemoth from that war, Fort Casey. The beautiful Admirality Head Lighthouse shares grounds with the fort, which has been partly restored. A ferry to Port Townsend leaves from a slip adjacent to Fort Casey State Park.

South of the reserve, the road flows through farmland that has been worked by the same families since it was first settled. Rolling hills with pleasing barns and farmhouses sport wheat, cattle, berries, and grapes, among other agricultural bounty. Greenbank and Freeland are towns that make small town life look very attractive indeed.

To return to the mainland at Mukilteo, speed vacationers should head west on Washington Highway 525 to the ferry terminal at Clinton. Clinton is a thirty-minute boat ride from Mukilteo. But those who want to stretch out their island retreat should turn west at Freeland and visit South Whidbey State Park. Or turn north off Highway 525 on Langley Road to visit Langley, another small town built on a bluff and supported by arts and charm.

SAN JUAN
Anacortes to Roche Harbor

For at least two thousand years before western explorers arrived, peoples from the Lummi, Samish, and Songish tribes paddled to the San Juan Islands in summer to fish, gather food, and hunt whales. San Juan Island is located in the rain shadow of Vancouver Island and the Olympic Mountain Range, and so enjoys more sunshine than the mainland to the west. It has the perfect weather and sheltered harbors for pleasure boating. For those who own pleasure cruising craft, there are eleven marine parks in this chain, with five on undeveloped islands perfect for re-enacting the film *Cast Away*.

ROUTE 8

From Anacortes, take the Washington State Ferry to San Juan Island's Friday Harbor. From there, drive south on San Juan Valley Road. Turn left on Douglas Road, then turn left on Madden Lane or Little Road to connect with Cattle Point Road.

Follow Cattle Point Road north, then turn left at Little Road, left on Douglas Road, and right on Bailer Hill Road, which becomes West Side Road. Follow West Side Road north, then turn right on Mitchell Bay Road and left on West Valley Road.

Follow West Valley Road north; it will become Roche Harbor Road and lead you into Roche Harbor.

Follow Roche Harbor Road back to Friday Harbor.

Unsung heroines, these women worked as rivet heaters and passers in the Puget Sound Navy Yard in 1919.

San Juan Island's Friday Harbor fills with pleasure boats, especially on sunny summer weekends.

Modern-day life on San Juan Island is governed by ferry schedules, including those of international routes that go to Sidney on Vancouver Island, Canada. For that reason, ferry boarding may be slowed for security checks. Fees for the trip will vary depending on the type of vehicle and the number of passengers included. Pay attention to boarding instructions given by the crew. Schedules may change according to weather, vacation traffic, and other factors. Washington State Ferries operates websites with current schedules and webcams for those who wish to avoid congested runs. Ferries are lifelines to the islands and stop at all the main ones along their routes, making a ferry trip longer than the map distance suggests. They travel through small straits and passages among the whole San Juan Island group, including private islands, marine park islands, and those too small to be of interest to any but seals and birds.

San Juan Island is the second largest in the island chain of the same name, but it is the most populated. The dock at Friday Harbor offers a happy taste of island life, with fine food, art, museums, views, and boat moorage. Four destinations are popular here and all are on the west face of the island. At the southern tip is American Camp, along Cattle Point Road. Drive south from Friday Harbor on San Juan Valley Road, turn left on Douglas Road headed south, and look for left turns onto Madden Lane or Little Road to connect with Cattle Point Road.

San Juan Island is the site of a "Pig War" with the British in the 1850s. In a rush to colonize, the border between British and American settlements was hotly contested, with the Hudson Bay Company having a post on San Juan Island, not far from a settlement of Americans. When a pig escaped from the Hudson Bay enclave and was shot by an American farmer, sabers were rattled. Encampments were fortified. But no more pigs or people were harmed and the border was established in 1871. Visitors love to roam the large parks that preserve the old settlements. American Camp has two preserved Pig War–era buildings and information about the war.

Drivers continuing north along the coast will see the beautiful Lime Kiln Point Lighthouse and stop to watch for whales traversing Haro Strait. Proceed north on Cattle Point road and turn west (left) at Little Road, south (left) on Douglas Road, and west (right) on Bailer Hill Road, which becomes West Side Road. Watch for left turns to Lime Kiln Point and Whale Watch Park.

English Camp and the Hudson Bay outpost are on West Valley Road beneath Young Hill, elevation 650 feet. From Lime Kiln Point, drive north on West Side Road, turn right on Mitchell Bay Road and left on West Valley Road. Historic buildings, as well as a small formal garden and gracious grounds, are preserved here.

For a taste of the "Gatsby" life, drive north on West Valley Road until it becomes Roche Harbor Road. Continue on to Roche Harbor, where the old Hotel de Haro and private marina are favorites among yacht owners.

At sunset, it is customary in the marina to shoot cannon and play bag-pipes. The bar is very civilized.

To connect with ferries back to Anacortes, simply follow Roche Harbor Road back to Friday Harbor. Come to think of it, if there is a tent in the trunk, or a vacancy at an island bed and breakfast, there is no rush to get back on the ferry. A little "island time" is an excellent antidote to a hectic personal schedule. A yacht is not necessary to enjoy pleasant afternoons on San Juan Island.

ORCAS ISLAND
Deer Harbor to Doe Bay

In 1791, Spanish explorer Francisco Eliza discovered the San Juan Island group and named them for his patron, the viceroy of Mexico. Orcas is the largest of the San Juan Islands, at fifty-eight square miles, and it has forty-five hundred year-round residents.

This route presumes reaching Anacortes by Highway 20 and heading west by ferry, disembarking at Orcas Island. Arrive at the ferry well ahead of your intended boarding time, because this run is on an international route to Sidney, British Columbia, and security measures may cause delays that extend to several hours. Attend to instructions when boarding with your car. Then get out of the car and begin enjoying the ride.

The passage to Orcas Island will take over an hour, because the ferry stops at two other islands along the way. Watch ferry docking at Lopez (consider getting off to look around but there are no public overnight accommodations), and then at Shaw Island. The tiny dock at Shaw is peaceful and rustic. A car and passengers can get off the ferry at either of the islands and re-board it with no additional fares.

Orcas Island is next. The island is shaped like a pair of saddlebags. The ferry docks at Orcas Village, located at the bottom of the right saddlebag. Drive north on Orcas Road and take a left turn on Deer Harbor Road. This part of the byway goes around the West Sound to Deer Harbor. Three marine parks, accessible only by boat, can be seen on this side of the island. Moorage is available in the towns of West Sound and Deer Harbor.

From Deer Harbor, backtrack on Deer Harbor Road and turn left on Crow Valley Road (a.k.a. Horseshoe Highway) to the town of Eastsound. This town has all services, including an airport. Point Doughty Recreation Area is just west of Eastsound, but it can only be reached by water.

On Main Street in Eastsound, drive southeast to connect with Olga Road (it's a right turn) and drive along the shore of the East Sound. Before you reach the entrance to Moran State Park, there is a turnoff to Rosario Road and the Rosario Resort on Cascade Bay. This venerable resort, spa, and marina got its beginnings when Robert Moran, a civic leader in Seattle, built a mansion to pass what he thought would be his last year of life. (Fortunately for him, medical predictions were wrong.) The elegant

ROUTE 9

From Anacortes, take the Washington State Ferry to Orcas Island. From Orcas Village, drive north on Orcas Road and turn left on Deer Harbor Road. Follow it until it reaches Deer Harbor.

From Deer Harbor, backtrack on Deer Harbor Road and turn left on Crow Valley Road, also known as Horseshoe Highway. Follow it to the town of Eastsound, then turn right on Olga Road and follow it south to a junction with Point Lawrence Road and Obstruction Pass Road. Follow Point Lawrence Road to Doe Bay, or follow Obstruction Pass Road to Obstruction Pass Park.

To return to Orcas Village, either retrace your route or turn left off Olga Road onto McNallie Lane, which becomes Dolphin Bay Road. Turn left on Killebrew Lake Road and follow it to the ferry dock.

ABOVE:

Entire pods of orcas take the Haro Strait passage between the Straits of Georgia and the Strait of Juan de Fuca.

RIGHT:

The San Juan Islands abound with wildlife. Eagle watching on Orcas Island is highly rewarding.

ABOVE:

A climb to the top of Mount Constitution rewards travelers with a view of Lummi, Clark, and Barnes Islands, and the mainland to the north.

LEFT:

Hospitality is one of the most significant products on Orcas Island. This delightful bed and breakfast offers meals and snacks with a view of the ferry dock.

old home has morphed into a luxurious resort with a full schedule of activities. Seaplane connections are available here.

Continuing south on Olga Road, look for signs and a left turn to Moran State Park. This five-thousand-acre destination is popular with vacationers. They like to swim in Mountain Lake, climb Mount Constitution (elevation 2,407 feet), trail bike, kayak, and watch whales. The view from Mount Constitution, the tallest point in the San Juan Islands, is big! This park also has camping, boat moorage, and an environmental learning center.

A pod of orcas called the "J Pod" spends its summers feeding in the waters of the San Juan Island chain. One of the most attractive pastimes for Orcas Island visitors is to take a whale-watching charter to see these remarkable creatures. Adventurous travelers can rent kayaks for an even closer view of the orcas. The animals' scientific name, *Orcianus Orca*, means "belonging to the realm of the dead." Local tribes saw the animals as a source of power. They portrayed beautiful stylized motifs of the orca on clan crests, and hunted them for food and materials to make weapons, tools, and art. Historically, sailors believed any encounter with "killer whales" to be deadly. Modern travelers see orcas as a source of wonder.

Each pod, or extended family group, has a favorite route and feeding area, fairly easy to locate and observe. Mike Sedam once watched the whales in J Pod breach and spy hop, cavort and splash, appearing to extend their interactions to the ferry full of enchanted humans.

Four orca calves were sighted in J Pod in 2004. Their orange baby skin is easy to spot in the center of a family escort. The calves will stay with J Pod throughout their lives, even after attending occasional convergences with K and L Pods near their island home. The little ones will also learn their pod's dialect—up to fifteen calls unique to their group.

Leaving the park, drive south on Olga Road; continue to a junction with Point Lawrence Road and Obstruction Pass Road. Take them both! Point Lawrence Road (left) passes picturesque Doe Bay on the way to Eagle Lake. Obstruction Pass Road (right) leads to Obstruction Pass Park and fine views of Obstruction Pass and Obstruction Island.

To return to Orcas Village and the ferry dock, retrace the route to Eastsound or turn left off Orcas Road onto McNallie Lane, which becomes Dolphin Bay Road. Proceed south past Diamond and Killebrew Lakes. Turn left on Killebrew Lake Road to return to the ferry dock.

Many adults in the cities on Puget Sound hold a soft spot in their hearts for Orcas Island because they attended summer camps there as children. In summer, camp busses and occasional swarms of children are to be expected. Bicyclers, likewise, come in flocks to enjoy the island routes. (It is possible to travel this backroad route by bicycle.) And places with names like Deer Harbor, Buck Park, and Doe Bay may be expected to be teeming with deer. Drive carefully. There's really no reason to hurry anyway.

THE PUGET SOUND COASTLINE
Mount Vernon to Bellingham

This backroad is practically a spring requirement for residents of the large cities in the Puget Sound region. Nowhere else do horticulture, harbor, and hairpin turns produce so much satisfaction.

Natives ply this route in March and April for the dazzling fields of daffodils, tulips, and iris, which are grown for their bulbs and exported all over the world. In order to produce the healthiest bulbs, the blossoms are routinely cut off just before the flowers peak, but the annual Tulip Festival in April celebrates their arrival anyway.

If you never get much farther than the broad, fifteen-square-mile flood plain that stretches between Mount Vernon and La Conner, you will be in bliss enough. Every year seven hundred to one thousand acres of outrageous color attract visitors desperately seeking signs of spring. Pick up a tulip brochure map at the Tulip Office and Museum, near exit 226 off Interstate 5, to find the most spectacular fields and tulip farm display areas. On especially good days of bloom, there are nearly as many cameras per acre as tulips. Gawking is the game here, so be sure to watch out for vehicles making unexpected stops (the views are that stunning) as well as bicyclists who love to tour this flat basin. Farm vehicles and the occasional livestock herd are other common obstacles.

At the west side of the Skagit Valley where McLean Road ends, turn left on La Conner–Whitney Road and head south to the picture postcard harbor town of La Conner. This is where local couples escape to romantic bed and breakfasts, especially in the rainy winter months. In summer, the protected waterway attracts boating enthusiasts. If shopping is your sport, this town also satisfies. The culinary arts are not neglected here either; restaurants, grand and casual, feature fresh seafood and local farm products. Opposite the town, across a graceful red bridge, is the Swinomish Indian Reservation, with its fleet of fishing boats.

Art lovers are drawn to the thriving colony of painters and craftsmen and the town's cultural centerpiece, the Museum of Northwest Art. Here resides a permanent collection of work by regional masters such as Mark Tobey, Kenneth Callahan, Morris Graves, and Paul Horiuchi. Numerous galleries display the work of other local artists.

Once filled up on blossoms and breakfast, leave La Conner and turn left on La Conner–Whitney Road. Continue north until the junction with Highway 20 and a stoplight. (Cross traffic will be drivers making their way to scenic Anacortes.) Turn right on Highway 20 and drive east back to Interstate 5. Get on the freeway going north but drive only to the next exit (231). Travel northwest to reach the road-building feat that is Chuckanut Drive, which shares an exit to Bow and Edison.

Drive across another few miles through rich green farmland until you arrive at the edge of Samish Bay. Here the road leaves the flatland,

ROUTE 10

From Mount Vernon, take Interstate 5 to exit 226 and head east on McLean Road. Turn left on La Conner–Whitney Road, heading south to La Conner (via a short stretch of Chiliberg Road). From La Conner, backtrack with a left turn onto La Conner–Whitney Road and turn right on Highway 20. Return to Interstate 5, then take exit 231, heading northwest on Chuckanut Drive. Follow it to Bellingham, via the old town district of Fairhaven.

RIGHT:
A harbinger of spring for sun-hungry residents of the Puget Sound is the tulip bloom and Tulip Festival in the Skagit Valley.

BELOW:
Rows of red blooms, as far as visible, point toward the western horizon and the hills of Fidalgo Island.

LEFT:

Although better known for tulips, Skagit Valley bulb growers also produce daffodil and iris bulbs for export.

HORSESHOE BEND - Chuckanut Drive
A Clyde Banks PHOTO 32

Workers chipped the engineering marvel Chuckanut Drive from solid rock hillsides in 1896 to connect Mount Vernon and Bellingham. Horseshoe Bend still requires careful navigation.

near a small oyster farm, and hauls up rock cliffs that tower above the salt water.

In ages past, ice fields hundreds of feet thick scoured this area, leaving rounded tops and contours on the forested slopes we travel today. But the ice met its match in solid rock hills, which now host scenic Washington Highway 11 (Chuckanut Drive). The road construction wasn't easy, and there was no option for a straight, speedy passage. Wind carefully over the next twenty-two miles, taking time to pull out at rustic stone-hemmed stopping places to view nearby islands. Steep drops make the beautiful coves below inaccessible and all the more covetous. To grasp the pace of this backroad, think of raccoon fur–coated college students from nearby Western Washington College touring at leisure in 1920s roadsters.

Approaching the end of Chuckanut Drive, look for the gracious stone gate that marks the entrance to Fairhaven Park. Also note the beginning of Bellingham's system of interurban trails that allow ambitious walkers and cyclists to travel across town without sharing space with cars.

The cliffs give way to the town of Bellingham, or more specifically, the old town district of Fairhaven. Brick buildings from the early heyday of cannery barons and timber merchants have been refurbished into stylish coffeehouses, bookstores, and boutiques. University students and professors populate the local cafés.

By turning downhill toward the bay on the main road through Fairhaven, arrive at the modern southern terminal for the Alaska Marine Highway. This is the jumping-off place for car and passenger trips up the Inland Passage to points north. Feel the pull that the wild places have on the backpackers waiting to board ferries to Alaska.

Drive up the hill again on Fairhaven Parkway to connect with Interstate 5 and return south to make a circuit back to Mount Vernon. This backroad route is just over thirty miles from Mount Vernon to Fairhaven but offers every pleasant kind of encounter with Puget Sound. From river valley to lazy saltwater slough, rock cliff to historic port, this drive features enough diversions to engage ramblers for a Sunday afternoon drive or a weekend out of town.

MOUNT BAKER
Glacier to Artist Point

This route is included in the Puget Sound region because it was from these waters that early European explorers first saw the prominent mountain. Mount Baker was named for Lieutenant Joseph Baker, who pointed it out from the deck of Captain George Vancouver's sloop *Discovery* near the San Juan Islands. Mount Baker is easier for Westerners to pronounce than the name given to the live volcano by the Nooksack Indians: *quck-sman-ik* or "white mountain."

Today, snow sports enthusiasts strap on skis or snowboards and glide down Baker's slopes over bases that have set world records for annual snowfall. It's a white mountain, indeed, which is why this road is not always open, even in summer. Check road conditions before starting on this route.

Start in the town of Glacier, mainly because there is a public service center there, run by the U.S. Forest Service, with information on the road ahead. Savvy drivers check their gas supply at Kendall, about ten miles before Glacier on Washington Highway 542. Those who plan hikes in the Mount Baker Wilderness Area or the Snoqualmie National Forest will want to stop at the center for permits.

From Glacier, this byway utilizes the Mount Baker Highway, heading east along the north fork of the Nooksack River towards closer views of the white mountain. Douglas Fir Campground is just outside of town on the right; rafting and snowmobile trips are staged from here. On the left is an appealing side trip on Forest Road 39, along Glacier Creek, to the outstanding view at Mount Baker Vista.

About five miles from Glacier, on Forest Road 37, is the Boyd Creek Interpretive Trail, with a self-guided tour emphasizing fish habitat. At seven miles from town, find a turnoff onto Wells Creek Road 33 to Nooksack Falls. There the Nooksack River hurtles over a one-hundred-foot drop amid luxurious green flanks.

ROUTE 11

From Glacier, follow the Mount Baker Highway (Washington Highway 542) east twenty-five miles to its terminus at Artist Point. Along the way, take side trips off the highway on Forest Roads 39, 37, 3065, and 32, as well as Wells Creek Road.

Mount Shuksan reflects in a mountain tarn. The growing season is brief but vigorous in alpine habitat.

A short hike to Artist Point offers this majestic view of Mount Baker.

LEFT:

The spotted owl thrives in old-growth areas such as Mount Baker National Forest.

Thirteen miles from Glacier are turnoffs for the Silver Fir Campground on the right and the Shuksan Picnic Area and Twin Lakes (Forest Road 3065) on the left, providing access along the Swamp Creek Drainage to the lakes. A gold rush started here in 1897 and mining activity continues to this day. Just beyond the Shuksan Picnic Area is a left exit, Forest Road 32, to Hannegan Pass, a favorite route for cross-country skiers. The same road provides access to Goat Mountain, where one of the area's four bands of mountain goats pastures in summer.

The last ten miles of this byway climb 3,200 feet from the Nooksack River to the side of Table Mountain. The road has switchbacks and steep banks and requires attentive driving. Just a couple miles past the Goat Mountain exit are splendid views of nearby Mount Shuksan (9,131 feet) and Mount Serfit (7,191 feet).

The Mount Baker Highway travels through a recreation complex beloved by winter sports fans. The Mount Baker Ski Area White Salmon Day Lodge accommodates mountain bikers, hikers, skiers, snowboarders, and sightseers. In the winter, the cleared portion of the road ends here.

One mile beyond the ski areas is the entrance to Heather Meadows, site of the first lodge on Mount Baker. A mile farther, find shoulder parking for access to Picture Lake. Heather Meadows and Picture Lake face Mount Shuksan and offer calendar-worthy views. Wild Goose and Bagley Lakes Trailheads are in the recreation area. Two lodges (a third is not open to the public), a picnic area, and a mountain shop provide services for mountain recreation. The Austin Pass Picnic Area and the Heather Meadows Visitor Center invite visitors to enjoy glorious views, attend naturalists programs, or use self-guided interpretive trails.

The end of the byway is Artist Point, elevation 5,140 feet. The parking area for this terminus does not do justice to the views that can be reached by short easy hikes. The Artist Ridge Trail is almost a mile long, but it rewards with astounding views of Mount Baker, Mount Shuksan, and Table Mountain. Artist Point is also the starting place for numerous hikes deep into the Snoqualmie National Forest and Mount Baker Wilderness Area. And it does inspire artists.

There are five live volcanoes in the Cascade Range in Washington State. Mount Baker is the only one with a ski area on its side. Sherman Crater, in the cone of the mountain, still vents steam and sulfur and, in fact, has stepped up that activity since 1975. Six notable mudflows have occurred since 1958; Mount Baker is considered the most active volcano in the Cascades after Mount Saint Helens. Though it is only 10,781 feet in elevation, it shoulders massive snowfall and glaciers by scraping rain from clouds from the Pacific Ocean. Mount Baker presents a unique geologic and ecologic environment that just happens to appeal to lots of outdoor sports enthusiasts.

The view from Mount Baker's slopes has always attracted visitors. This climbing party, in 1906, was properly outfitted for a day of mountain exploration. (Courtesy of the Washington State Historical Society)

PART III

THE
CASCADE MOUNTAINS

FACING PAGE:
Lake Eunice can be reached by a short hike from Mowich Lake, a walk-in campground at the end of the Carbanado byway.

ABOVE:
Tree fruit farmers greet the new year's crop with its spring display of blossoms. These blooms are apple.

"Plate tectonics" is a phrase that gets use on the west coast of North America. In Washington, evidence of movement within the earth's crust is most visible in the Cascade Range, a row of mountains stretching north and south from Canada to Mexico. This rugged chain of mountains, incorporating numerous live volcanoes, reflects the stress of subduction between the Juan de Fuca Plate and the North American Plate. Washington State has five live volcanoes and evidence of myriad others, which were active as the seafloor was pushed up to make mountains. The resulting formation divides the state into distinct weather zones with implications for population, economics, lifestyle, and even political preferences.

The Cascade Range has inspired ingenious engineering feats to puncture the barrier for trade and transportation. Bridges, tunnels, roads, snow and avalanche control, river and air travel have perforated the mountain range in an attempt to stitch the state together. The practical problems of crossing this range are well known to residents. Trips "over the pass" require preparation, reliable transportation, and two or three hours of travel. Winter is especially problematic because the Cascade Range draws precipitation from clouds moving west off the Pacific Ocean, and that means lots of snow. Keeping mountain roads open is a tough, vital business.

And then there are those volcanoes. In 1980, Mount Saint Helens erupted, distributing its peak worldwide. Now it is rebuilding its conical form. Towns and villages below Mount Rainer practice evacuation drills to prepare for potentially catastrophic eruptions. Reservoirs below Mount Baker have systems to lower their water levels if the white landmark above them should erupt. Mount Adams is considered less of a threat to populations, and Glacier Peak is in a remote wilderness, but they still garner respect and study.

The Cascade Mountains are a vast laboratory for paleontologists and naturalists. They also yield treasures of minerals for prospectors and trees for timber interests. But the industry that is flourishing the most in these mountains is recreation. Fans are drawn to these beautiful, accessible mountains year-round for physical and spiritual adventures. Active travelers may employ equipment and facilities that change with technology and trends, but the objective stays the same: Humans enter these regions to connect with something huge. They come away with a better understanding of priorities and bond with others in the process.

So now, quick before something erupts, get started on your own connections. Motor up to live volcanoes, climb their sides, and ski down them. Rumble through wildernesses remote enough to prompt grizzly bear warnings. Visit lakes and streams carrying cold water from the snow-capped peaks to the towns and valleys below. Encounter old, deep green forests and learn about the animals that live in them. Drive on roads built on migration paths blazed by the earliest peoples, and exercise your inner pioneer in towns that re-create the early days of western settlement.

OVERLEAF:
Glacial silt heightens the color of beautiful Diablo Lake, on the North Cascades Highway.

Haul up a tent, a canoe, a mountain bike, a llama, a snowboard, a fishing pole, a rock hammer, a camera, a compass, a snowmobile, a field guide, a rain poncho, and an appetite for adventure. The Cascades Mountains are alive and waiting to accommodate.

NORTH CASCADES
Winthrop to Sedro-Woolley

ROUTE 12
─────────────

Beginning at the town of Winthrop, drive west on Washington Highway 20 (the North Cascades Highway). Follow it 130 miles through the towns of Mazama, Diablo, Newhalem, Marblemount, Rockport, Concrete, Hamilton, and Lyman, ending at Sedro-Woolley.

Winthrop is one of those places that encourage John Wayne imitations. Its western frontier theme is persistent and fun! The Methow River meets the Chewuch River, along with Washington Highway 20, also known as the North Cascades Highway. Motor on to the North Cascades Scenic Highway Visitor Center or the Methow Valley Ranger Station, pilgrim, where this backroad begins. A side trip to Pearrygin Lake might be in order if the day is hot or if fishing enthusiasts are in the wagon.

Highway 20 follows the Methow River north into the Cascade Mountains and into North Cascades National Park. The park was established in 1968 and the highway was opened in 1972. This byway takes travelers through spectacular mountain scenery. From about mid November to mid April, Mazama is the end of the road. Because weather conditions vary so much from year to year, it's a good idea to call the National Park Service to check road conditions in April and again in late September. Be sure to check the gas gauge, too, because it's about fifty miles between stations on this part of the highway.

There's a campground at Mazama and another, Early Winters, a couple miles farther. Shortly after that, you embark on the part of Highway 20 that has been named a Washington State Scenic Byway. The Cedar Creek Trailhead is another couple miles farther and close to the Kipchuck Campground.

The road gains altitude as it leaves the Methow River Valley. Note signs for Lone Fir Campground and Cutthroat Trailhead just before the final climb to the pass. The road curves south along Kangaroo Ridge, then comes to the face of Liberty Bell Mountain. It looks like a hopeless ascent, but intrepid road builders have created a winding hill climb that goes around the behemoth at Washington Pass (5,477 feet). A ranger station there points out features. The views from the bottom and the top of this highway section require a sense of wonder.

Rainy Pass is a short way beyond Washington Pass and has picnic facilities, wheelchair access to Rainy Lake, and the beginning of a system of trails that leads to the Lake Chelan Recreation Area. From here, the highway descends on the Granite Creek drainage until it meets with Ruby Creek near the main body of Ross Lake. This reservoir, created by Seattle City Light to provide about 25 percent of the city's electricity needs, is a teal blue, glacier-fed jewel. It extends into British Columbia, with boating, hiking, and camping sites along its eastern shores.

The highway follows the Ruby Arm of the lake around Ruby Mountain, which has a world-class overlook where drivers can stop to see what their passengers are raving about. If you plan ahead, you can book tickets for the famous Seattle City Light boat tour of the lake.

Highway 20 continues toward Diablo Lake, passing the Happy Creek Forest Walk and a Diablo Lake Overlook. Stop again and fire up your camera to capture the spectacular view. Diablo has limited services and is where those Skagit Tours begin.

From the Diablo exit, continue on to Newhalem, where there are gas and recreation services. Just west of town are two campgrounds—Goodell Creek and Newhalem—and the North Cascades Visitor Center.

Highway 20 follows the Skagit River from Diablo all the way to Sedro-Woolley, 130 miles from Winthrop. Marblemount, west of Newhalem, has a North Cascades National Park Wilderness Information Center where backcountry permits are available. The next seventeen miles between

Fruit crate labels were the original "point of purchase" advertising. Growers and packers used topical names, graphics, and product claims to encourage sales. This 1930s label echoes President Roosevelt's enthusiasm for the New Deal programs.

This mountain stream crosses the roadway on the North Cascades Highway and flows into Diablo Lake.

This cowboy rides a little stiff in the saddle. Photo opportunities abound on the streets of Winthrop.

Visitors enjoy the boardwalks in western-style Winthrop. Town merchants have ingeniously adopted the theme for their businesses.

Newhalem celebrates its history with a preserved steam locomotive at the town's entrance. This engine was used in the construction of the Ross and Diablo Dams.

A cowboy earns his paycheck at the Winthrop rodeo. An annual cattle drive takes range herds through the middle of town.

Marblemount and Concrete are famous as wintering grounds for the largest population of bald eagles in the lower forty-eight states. You can find them perched in trees, looking for salmon in the river.

Marblemount, Rockport, and Concrete passed their heydays in the late 1800s, but still function as gateways to North Cascade Range passages for prospectors, tribe members, and adventuresome travelers. Concrete sits below Lower Baker Dam and Lake Shannon, and serves a cluster of campgrounds on the Baker Lake Highway to the north.

The North Cascades Highway arrives in the ever-widening lower Skagit River Valley, passing Hamilton and Lyman on the way to Sedro-Woolley. This logging community showcases its heritage with an annual Loggerodeo. The visitor information center is a real 1913 steam engine heading up a logging car and a caboose. Murals, logging equipment, large wooden carvings, steam train rides, a buffalo farm, and a history museum attest to this town's pride in its past. The town also has a ranger station to dispense information for those approaching the highway from the west.

About 93 percent of the North Cascades National Park was declared part of the Stephen Mather Wilderness Area in 1988. This wild gem adjoins a wilderness area in Canada to yield a vast protected Eden where grizzlies and wolves still prowl. This backroad adventure reveals a tantalizing slice of what these creatures experience every day.

HIGH MOUNTAIN PASS
Monroe to Cashmere

ROUTE 13

To reach Monroe from Interstate 5, take Washington Highway 522 East. In Monroe, head east on U.S. Highway 2. You'll pass through the towns of Sultan, Startup, Gold Bar, Skykomish, and Cole's Corner. At Cole's Corner, turn left to visit Lake Wenatchee State Park. Backtrack to U.S. 2 and continue east to Leavenworth. Shortly after Leavenworth, U.S. 2 becomes U.S. Highway 97. Follow it to Cashmere.

Stevens Pass, otherwise known as U.S. Highway 2, is one of two year-round lifelines that stitch eastern and western Washington together (the other being Snoqualmie Pass, Interstate 90, to the south). Truckers, college students, vacationers, and outdoors adventurers are familiar with this beautiful backroad through the heart of the Cascade Mountain Range.

Travelers from Seattle know they have shed the city when they arrive in Monroe. This growing rural town features lush dairy farmland, a state penitentiary, and the Evergreen State Fair that convenes every fall. At Monroe the serious work of crossing a mountain range begins; many travelers stop for a meal at the town's new fast food district before they continue on.

U.S. 2 follows the Skykomish River up the mountains, where it is cradled, more and more deeply, by forested slopes and rocky crags. Small towns along the route serve tourism and survive brutal mountain winters. If there is any need for automotive services before assaulting the pass, be sure to complete them now.

Sultan has a beautiful picnic area alongside the river and shops to stock the picnic basket. The name of the next town, Startup, presages the climb to come. Gold Bar serves hamburgers and supplies for outdoor recreation enthusiasts. With each town, U.S. 2 heads deeper into the forested mountains.

East of Gold Bar, look for a sign to Wallace Falls State Park. Once in the park, exit your car and walk into a cool green forest of Douglas fir, hemlock, cedar, and alder, surrounded by a carpet of deep springy loam and dense undergrowth. Streams and rivulets frequently cross the trail. This is the way forests grow on the wet western slopes of the Cascade Mountains.

Back on U.S. 2, continue to the town of Skykomish. This is the "putting in" point for exhilarating rafting trips to Monroe on the Skykomish River. For those with backcountry plans in the Mount Baker–Snoqualmie National Forest (nearly everyone!) the ranger station in Skykomish issues permits and information.

The highway twists and climbs steeply past distant waterfalls and forested bowls to the top of Stevens Pass. Many don't plan to go any further than this popular recreation area. In summer, hiking, fishing, hunting, rock climbing, mountain biking, and horseback riding are all available. In winter, the place really gets busy. Skiers (downhill, cross-country, and helcat), show shoers, snowmobilers, and dog and downhill sledders get their turn. Lifts, equipment rentals, instructors, food, housing, and automobile needs, including chain-up services, await vacationers at the top of Stevens Pass.

So do rapidly changing weather conditions. It is not easy to keep a highway in the Cascade Mountains open all winter. Dial 511 and ask for mountain pass information or check the Web before driving the pass, and bring along chains and patience.

U.S. 2 descends quickly on the east side of the pass, bringing a significant change in the landscape. The thick forests of the western slopes give way to pine, tamarack, and occasional birch stands with sparse grass, sunflower, and sage undergrowth. Most of the year, the thin forest floors and treeless hillsides are brown. This is the look of the dry eastern side of the Cascade Range. For the next thirty miles, the road rolls through cowboy hillsides of weathered rock and trees. Look for the Bygone Byways Interpretive Trail to learn more about this region's earlier times.

At Cole's Corner, consider turning left for a side trip to glacier-fed Lake Wenatchee. The Nason Creek campground, on the way to the lake, is also inviting.

Back on the highway, the road drops into the Tumwater River canyon. The rocky walls that hold this tumbling river are made more austere by a recent forest fire that left snagged slopes to slowly re-grow. Still, winding through the cool stone canyon and the remaining tall pines, tamaracks, and vine maples is refreshing, especially in the autumn when the colors are high.

The highway emerges from the canyon into Leavenworth. Here is a successful alpine-themed village, enhanced by spectacular mountain backdrops and festivals for every season. It is also a jumping-off place for every kind of mountain recreation.

RIGHT:

Nason Creek, near Lake Wenatchee, shows the crystal beauty of winter waters.

BELOW:

The Bavarian-style village of Leavenworth, set within the Icicle and Entiat Mountains, turns up the wattage to celebrate Christmas. Yuletide events crown a year-round calendar of town festivals.

Adventure-seekers raft the white water at Boulder Drop near Index. This stretch of river is considered extremely challenging.

STREET SCENE · LEAVENWORTH · WN   AUGUST 1953

Before transforming itself into a Bavarian-themed tourist haven, Leavenworth was a struggling farm town, pictured here in 1953.

U.S. 2 becomes U.S. Highway 97 a few miles out of Leavenworth and follows the Wenatchee River. The valleys become broader, with orchard carpets. The town of Cashmere is close at hand. River rafters float under the bridges that admit tourists to this all-American town. The factory that makes and ships Applets and Cotlets (famous fruit candies) is located here, as well as a museum that features a pioneer village.

Turn back or go on to Wenatchee? The decision depends on the time of year. In early May, go on to Wenatchee and enjoy the Apple Blossom Festival.

MOUNT SAINT HELENS'S EAST SIDE
Randle to Windy Ridge

ROUTE 14

From U.S. Highway 12 in Randle, drive south on Washington Highway 131. Continue south as the highway becomes Forest Road 25. Follow signs to Forest Road 99 leading to Spirit Lake and Windy Ridge.

Randle is a small mountain town that probably would still be slumbering if the volcano next door hadn't awakened it in 1980. Now it is the starting place for a journey that approaches the Mount Saint Helens crater from the east side. Each side of Mount Saint Helens received a different effect from the blast that changed everything. The approach via Johnson Ridge (the next backroad route) shows what volcanic forces can do in the initial blast. This eastern approach features the wall of the volcanic cone that remained.

As you approach Randle from the west, Cowlitz Falls Campground tempts you with lakefront camping, fishing, and boating. Take a right on Peters Road if it's a hot summer day and you feel like giving in to those temptations.

Summer is the only time this road from Randle to Windy Ridge is accessible, and this trip starts at a shady tree-lined road then it enters the blow-down area of the Mount Saint Helens National Volcanic Monument. Heading south on Washington Highway 131, you enter the Gifford Pinchot National Forest, and the road becomes Forest Road 25. An information center near the boundary has current weather and trail conditions and permits. About fifteen miles from the center, look for a sign for Forest Road 99 to Spirit Lake and Windy Ridge. The road enters the Mount Saint Helens National Volcanic Monument about five miles from the turnoff to Forest Road 99.

The total driving distance from Randle to Windy Ridge is thirty-seven miles, but in awe miles, it's a lot farther. Alternate forest roads lead to the shore of Spirit Lake or bypass the Windy Ridge Viewpoint to connect with sites and activities on the south side of the volcano (Forest Road 25). These roads are generally open from Memorial Day until the first significant snowfall in the fall. They are paved or graded, gravel-topped passages that wind around the arms of the volcano. The views are often spectacular, but drivers need to watch for elk, deer, and other gawking drivers. Significant sites are marked with pullouts, interpretive signs, and short self-guided hikes. There are no gas stations on this route after leaving Randle.

That said, this road takes advantage of a natural disaster to show travelers the forest that was formerly hidden by the trees. It offers an entirely different view of volcanic violence than that of the northwestern route to Johnson Ridge. A bonus is that occasional pullouts offer views of other live volcanoes in the Cascade Range. Mount Rainier, the majestic volcano to the north, is well displayed in clear-cut areas along the route. Mount Adams, to the east, is also prominent, and in good weather, the tipsy stack of Mount Hood across the Columbia River in Oregon is visible as well.

Spirit Lake was once a beautiful, blue, summer-cabin heaven, full of fish and surrounded by tall fir trees. Pictures of the lake, pre-eruption, show people fishing from canoes, swimming, and picnicking in shady groves. Forest Road 99 skirts the edge of Spirit Lake, coming close to the shore at the north and south end. A viewpoint over the lake gives an understated picture of pyroclastic violence. It now looks like a valley of logs, surrounded by bare hills. The lake is nearly covered with a raft of logs that still drift with the wind twenty years after they fell. The eruption filled the southern shore with mudflow. The shockwave blew down surrounding forests as if they were toothpicks and pushed much of the timber from the north slope of the volcano into the lake. The heat of the blast left some hillsides along the lake simply charred black. Amazingly, the eruption spared the lake's frogs and fish, which seem to thrive today.

Now Forest Road 99 climbs up the side of the volcano. In these heights, areas of blow-down have been left untouched and still inspire contemplation. Looking to the east, along the Smith Creek drainage, islands of thick

This 1940s travel brochure advertises Mount Saint Helens and Spirit Lake as a green vacation paradise. The view from this shore would be unrecognizable following the mountain's 1980 eruption.

Life returns to the blasted earth twenty-five years after Mount Saint Helens violently erupted. Wildflowers venture into open spaces, offering their color notes to bare rock.

FACING PAGE, BOTTOM:

The shores of Spirit Lake offer plenty of driftwood benches. Mount Saint Helens's most recent eruption covered much of the lake with a raft of blown-down logs.

ABOVE:

Just outside the Volcano Monument, a mountain stream hints at the kind of habitat that surrounded Mount Saint Helens before it roared to life.

Company #933 C.C.C. near Randle, Wash.
7/19/33 — #318

The Civilian Conservation Corp offered room, board, and work for young men under the New Deal and provided crews for public projects land reclamation. Company No. 933, housed at Randle, poses in midsummer 1933 at their new camp. (Courtesy of the Washington State Historical Society)

green exist amid hillsides of scoured soil and bristles of dead trees. Eagles have learned to take advantage of this landscape for soaring and hunting. On hot summer days, fine ash still swirls from the hillsides, which are now beginning to sport green shrubbery and wildflowers.

The road ends on aptly named Windy Ridge, at a magnificent viewpoint with parking, toilets, and interpretive material. In clear weather, the new dome forming in the middle of the crater is clearly visible, and winds pick up ash from the bowl and vault it into the sky. Awesome.

One of the greatest pleasures of staying alive is seeing and understanding paramount phenomena—from a safe viewpoint. Windy Ridge is just such a place. There are five live volcanoes in Washington's portion of the Cascade Mountain Range, and all of them hold the potential to behave as this one did in 1980. Even as the landscape begins to heal, more than twenty years later, it is good to remember the possibilities. An afternoon in the face of a sleeping giant ought to do it.

MOUNT SAINT HELENS'S WEST SIDE
Castle Rock to Johnson Ridge

Moments after Mount Saint Helens erupted on May 18, 1980, miles of fresh, fertile mountain landscape were altered forever. This route takes travelers past a variety of consequences, following the North Fork of the Toutle River to a vantage point that offers a panorama of the magnificent damage so quickly done. Prepare to be awed by the scale of this cataclysm.

Start at Interstate 5 in Castle Rock. There is no visible result of the volcano here except for the Cinedome Theater, which shows "The Eruption" several times a day, and the Harry Truman Memorial Park. Castle Rock also has an exhibit hall featuring logging history.

Take exit 49 and head east on the Spirit Lake Memorial Highway—an award-winning route offering lessons in geology and ecology.

Five miles east, a Mount Saint Helens visitor center operated by the Northwest Interpretive Association (NIA) offers another learning opportunity; it is the first of three private, fee-charging NIA facilities along the route. Continue east to reach Sequest State Park, popular with summer campers and boaters for its access to beautiful Silver Lake. The highway passes the north side of the lake to show off pleasing wooded hills and sparkling waters rich with bass.

Shortly after leaving the lakeside, you will arrive in the town of Toutle, where all services and camping supplies are available. From here on, the highway follows the North Fork of the Toutle River almost to its point of origin at Spirit Lake. At Toutle River, you can connect with Highway 504; this is something of a shortcut for travelers from the cities on Puget Sound. Local tree farms boast verdant vigor on cool hillsides. The small town of Kid Valley provides the last opportunity to fill gas tanks for the next sixty-five miles.

Twenty miles from Interstate 5, watch for a sign to the Sediment Retention Structure. This holding basin was built to control future volcanic run-off, using lessons learned from the 1980 event. At Hoffstadt Bluff Visitor Center (free), see how this knowledge was gained. Hoffstadt Bluff stands at the edge of the tree blow-down area. The Toutle River here has gone wide and gray with ash, rock, and timber that rushed down the mountain all the way to the Columbia River.

After Hoffstadt Bluff, the highway crosses Hoffstadt Creek over an elegant bridge, which has passing views of the blast zone. A few miles on, consider a stop at the free Forest Learning Center to learn about the use and rebirth of forests in the volcanic monument and the surrounding Gifford Pinchot National Forest. Near the learning center is the Elk Rock Viewpoint. It was the end of the public access road for many years after the eruption. Now the highway goes on over a 3,800-foot pass with

From Interstate 5 at Castle Rock, take exit 49 to Washington Highway 504, also called the Spirit Lake Memorial Highway. Drive east through Toutle and Kid Valley, arriving at the Johnson Ridge Observatory on the west side of the volcano.

The upper reaches of the Toutle River carve through mudflow at the base of Mount Saint Helens.

Elk populations have risen as the blasted landscape around Mount Saint Helens begins to grow browse plants. Herds are easy to spot from overlooks and visitor centers.

BELOW:

Visitors observe the blown-out core of Mount Saint Helens from the large patio at the visitor center at Johnson Ridge. It's the site for naturalists' lectures, binocular viewing, and camera clicking. A resident elk herd is often conveniently stationed in the valley below.

breathtaking views, before it dips downhill on the way to Johnson Ridge, the newest end of the road.

The NIA Coldwater Visitor Center sits near Coldwater Lake. This lake was created when the eruption dammed up Coldwater Creek. Picnic and boat-launching areas are available for day use.

The changes to the Mount Saint Helens landscape, for those who have watched it since 1980, are nothing short of a gratifying testament to the persistence of nature. However, the testament has been edited by timber salvage and replanting, exhaustive study, and diverse popular interests. At Loowit Viewpoint and Trailhead, a small area of untouched blowdown gives seekers a glimpse of the power of a volcano blast. *Loo-Wit* or "Keeper of Fire" was one of the names given to Mount Saint Helens by local tribes familiar with its eruptive ways. Now it is the name of a recreation area and a trail that encircles the crater.

About fifty miles from Interstate 5, arrive at the four-thousand-foot level and the NIA Johnson Ridge Observatory. The observatory offers a perfectly located point from which to view the lopsided crater and its emerging dome. Lots of information and short hikes to nearby viewpoints make this a popular learning site. Below, in the wide valley of pyroclastic devastation, tender new life sprouts in the nutritious volcanic soil. Herds of deer and elk roam in the new meadows. Spring flowers crowd the slopes. Alders and young evergreens have taken root in areas not specifically replanted with fir seedlings. Snow again caps the high rim each winter.

This 1914 photograph, taken at Peterson's Cave on the side of Mount Saint Helens, offers early evidence of the mountain's geologic volatility. Caves on the mountain's south side still attract hikers.

But the cratered moonscape of Mount Saint Helens still growls ominously. The baby dome in its center grows. Loo-Wit still needs to be watched.

CAYUSE PASS
Greenwater to Paradise Valley

Mount Rainier is an icon for the state of Washington. This live volcano released mudflows seventy feet deep into valleys twenty-four miles northwest of its summit during a seismic event fifty-eight hundred years ago. Today, those valleys are filled with towns and suburbs that enjoy stunning vistas of the very mountain that may inundate them again. This byway crosses the northeast slope of quiet-for-now Mount Rainier and follows a spectacular "summer only" pass to arrive at a special area in the national park.

Enumclaw, a town on Washington Highway 410 situated atop the ancient mudflow, is where mountain travelers can pick up permits and weather information about the passes ahead. The route actually begins eighteen miles east at Greenwater, within the Mount Baker–Snoqualmie National Forest, and the town is the last chance for gasoline for fifty-four miles. Here the road parallels the White River south and east onto the side of Rainier. Recreation sites and popular outdoor activities define this byway.

The nearby Federation Forest still bears wagon ruts from western migration on the Naches Trail. Interpretive material here explains the realities of the trips undertaken by thousands of hearty pioneer families. Envisioned by and named for the first director of the National Park Service, the Mather Memorial Parkway on Highway 410 begins near the turnoff to Bald Mountain (Forest Road 73).

Camping and hiking opportunities abound along Highway 410. There's The Dalles Campground on the glacier-silted White River, as well as Skookum Falls Campground, Camp Shepherd Trailhead, Buck Creek Recreation Area, and Silver Springs Campground. Highway 410 climbs steadily from here. Watch for a turnoff to the Crystal Mountain Ski Area, a sports facility offering a mountainside of skiing, snowboarding, and snowshoeing, among other activities.

Once you enter Mount Rainier National Park, old-growth trees crowd right up to the roadway dew line. Seven miles in, note the turnoff for White River campground and the famous Sunrise Lodge. Just beyond the White River turnoff, a rock-walled car pullout and a convenient recent avalanche makes possible a breathtaking panoramic view of the mountain in clear weather. This site is a short drive from the summit of Cayuse Pass, which rises 4,694 feet.

This route continues on the Cayuse Pass Highway (Washington Highway 123), but a beautiful alternative is to turn east, continuing to follow

ROUTE 16

From Greenwater, drive southeast on Washington Highway 410. At Cayuse Summit, take Washington Highway 123 South. At Stevens Canyon, turn right onto Washington Highway 706. Turn right about a mile and a half past Reflection Lake, enter Mount Rainier National Park, and continue following the road to Paradise.

These gossamer cascades are the namesake for Falls Creek, just a half mile inside the Mount Ranier National Park.

Paradise Valley was surely well named. In fall, leaves of mountain heather turn scarlet to frame Mount Rainier in glory before the first snowfall.

Climbing Mount Rainier has been a popular challenge ever since English explorer George Vancouver discovered the peak in 1792. These mountaineers, climbing in the early 1900s, take on Paradise Glacier in the newly established Mount Rainier National Park. (Courtesy of the Library of Congress)

the Mather Memorial Parkway to nearby Chinook Pass. Cayuse and Chinook are normally open only in the summer months and even that varies with annual weather conditions. Cayuse often opens in mid May and Chinook generally opens by Memorial Day. It's a good idea to check on access. If you stay on the Mather Memorial Highway, Lake Tipsoo is several miles beyond the Cayuse summit and begs for a moment with a camera. The drive follows Chinook Creek and then Ohanapecosh River to the national park's Stevens Canyon entrance. If you have the time, camp at Ohanapecosh Campground and Visitor Center on Highway 123 just past the park entrance. This enchanting campground is beautifully sited in an old-growth forest.

At the Stevens Canyon park entrance, turn right to drive to Paradise Valley. The road to the valley climbs above the Ohanapecosh River and around Backbone Ridge to reach Stevens Canyon. Then it passes striking mountain lakes: Bench, Louise, and wonderful Reflection Lake. The road hangs on to the side of Stevens Ridge and has tunnels and turnouts to accommodate increasingly amazing views of the Tatoosh Range and Mount Rainier.

Paradise is an appropriate name for the sub-alpine meadow area of this valley. Wildflowers garnish the meadows after spring snowmelt, and heather blooms in late summer. The lower valley has the Henry M. Jackson Memorial Visitor Center, and the upper valley has the Paradise Inn. There is no camping in Paradise Valley but there are other services, including mountain guides for those who wish to climb the 14,401-foot peak. Most visitors walk up the 1.2-mile Nisqually Vista Trail to the edge of the Nisqually Glacier. On a clear day, panoramas in any direction are inspiring.

James Longmire was an early entrepreneur who, in 1888, established a hotel on the mountain at Medical Springs in what is now the southwest corner of the national park. His daughter Martha named the valley, exclaiming when she saw it, "This must be what Paradise is like." Modern visitors would concur.

LEFT:

In 1919, makers of the "Detroit Electric" automobile drove it from Seattle to Mount Rainier to capture this glamour shot and demonstrate the vehicle's dependability.

BELOW:

A logging crew near the White River proudly poses with its steam "donkey," which provided the muscle to hoist logs, by a series of pulleys and a spar pole, onto wagons or skids for transport to rafts and mills.

This steel arch, an example of engineering elegance, spans a deep green canyon on Washington Highway 165 as it approaches the national park boundary.

An enduring and endearing road machine marks the entrance to Wilkeson, a town with historic roots.

A Wilkeson cemetery traces the struggles won and lost in this coal-mining town.

False-front architecture, typical of the boomtown days when coal mining was highly profitable, distinguishes these old stores on Washington Highway 165.

CARBONADO
Buckley to Mowich Lake

ROUTE 17

Begin in Buckley on Washington Highway 410. Drive southwest and take a left turn onto Highway 165, heading south to Wilkeson. After Carbonado, the highway splits. Take the fork to the right and enter Mount Rainier National Park. The road ends at a campsite alongside Mowich Lake.

In the late 1800s, when settlers began occupying the western territories, natural resources seemed to have infinite profit potential. Fuel for progress, in the form of coal deposits, occurs in abundance in western Washington; people such as Samuel Wilkeson, Jr., invested in coal mining and transportation empires and created boomtowns in the process. Other towns exploited their timber resources with similar results.

This backroad travels through some of those former boomtowns on the way to a more contemporary asset, a rustic recreational site and staging area for mountain appreciation of all kinds.

A town of forty-two hundred, Buckley is a timber settlement at the edge of the city sprawl around Puget Sound. Its annual Logger's Rodeo celebrates skills formerly needed to work here. Logging trucks still rumble along Highway 410, carrying harvests from the Cascade Mountains. However, Buckley has evolved to offer recreation equipment rentals and services as well. Drive south through town to the junction with Washington Highway 165 (look for signs to Wilkeson). On the way to Wilkeson pass the grocery store that is the town of Burnett.

Wilkeson was founded in 1880 and in only twenty years boasted a growing population of coal miners and their families. It was named for Samuel Wilkeson, Jr., the corporate board secretary of the Northern Pacific Railroad and prime investor in the Wilkeson Coal and Coke Company. The town was named for him as a present for his sixtieth birthday. He shipped coal, via the railroad, to supply iron refineries in Tacoma. Remnants of "uptown" Wilkeson, rows of identical company houses, still survive, as does a school built in 1913 and the oldest Orthodox Church in the lower forty-eight states.

Today, travelers purchase gas, water, and food in Wilkeson, since none are available at Mowich Lake. The Mount Rainier National Park Wilderness Information Center in town issues permits for park uses and answers questions.

Drive south on Highway 165 past Carbonado, another town with a coal surge in its history. In the 1930s, oil became the fuel of choice for transportation and lighting, and coal mining dwindled. Facing expensive safety requirements, Carbonado mines closed in 1974, with 98 percent of their deposits untapped. Now the town is a gateway to the national park, as well as the Snoqualmie National Forest and Clearwater Wilderness Area.

Out of Carbonado, the highway crosses a one-lane iron bridge over a deep rock canyon, with the Carbon River far below. Less than a mile from the bridge, you have two options. You can take the left fork in the road to reach the Carbon River entrance of the national park and the popular Ipsuit Campground. Since the access road to the campground seems to be in the bed of Ipsuit Creek, expect some bumpy going. Or you can turn right at the fork, climbing on unpaved roadway, passing the Evans Creek ORV area, and arriving at the Mowich Lake park entrance. A self-pay station collects fees from those who did not buy passes in Wilkeson.

Mount Rainier National Park protects mountainsides of lush green old-growth forest. On this route, private companies log areas just outside the park boundaries. The contrasts are dramatic, though the scraped hillsides do afford big views of the Carbon River Valley.

End your road trip at the parking lot for the Mowich Lake walk-in campground. No reservations are offered, and this primitive campground (chemical toilets and no water) is fully occupied on some sunny summer weekends. It is a stopover for hikers taking the Wonderland Trail, which winds around the entire mountain, as well as a starting point for numerous other popular trails within the park.

Mowich Lake itself is a beautiful sub-alpine waterway pocketed under Mother Mountain and Elizabeth Ridge. Its meadows burst with wildflowers after snowmelt. A small ranger's cabin shelters summer naturalists and rangers. It's safe to say a lot of cameras have clicked at this lake.

The Carbon Hill Coal Company pauses for a picture with renowned mine manager Robert Wingate, in the foreground, holding a child. Mules powered coal car transport from the mine to loading sites via light rail tracks. (Courtesy of the Washington State Historical Society)

PART IV

THE
COLUMBIA RIVER

FACING PAGE:

Crown Point, on the Columbia River Scenic Highway in Oregon, offers a panorama of the scenic river at sunset.

ABOVE:

A hearty windsurfer exploits the current and wind direction on the Columbia River near Hatchery Beach.

Woodie Guthrie wrote songs about the mighty Columbia River, celebrating the work of harnessing its power. The first peoples probably had songs, too, for this river that starts in the heart of the continent and grows until it breaches a mountain range to reach the sea. Nearly everyone living in Washington has some connection to this majestic waterway. From the food on our tables to the electricity in our homes, the Columbia supplies much.

What the Cascade Mountains divide in Washington State, this river conquers. Its drainage travels through two Canadian provinces and three inland states before it becomes the muscular force that curves across inland plateaus to divide Washington and Oregon. This river has prevailed over ice ages and droughts to sculpt enormous scablands and rock-walled canyons. It bestows fertility to farms growing every kind of foodstuffs, and a waterway to transport them to market. Its waters are home to salmon, a force in themselves, and efforts to restore their migration runs have consequences for every part of Washington and other parts of the river's drainage.

And when the Columbia reaches the Pacific Ocean, its influence is still prodigious. The mere rumor of the river brought explorers from the Old World, and the search for it divulged resources that changed nations. Those who sought the river mapped and renamed every significant landmark visible from their wooden ships. Meriwether Lewis and William Clark used the river, from its junction with the Snake River, as their primary route to the Pacific coast. To celebrate the bicentennial anniversary of their voyage of discovery, their campsites and journal entries are highlighted all along the river. Inland, the river dictated passageways across the hot plateau lands for tribes, traders, and settlers, as well as wild and domestic animal herds.

When the river, now grown to the largest on the west coast, reaches the sea, it continues to confer fertility on coastal waters, serving the seafood harvest as handily as the wheat harvest. Today, its channels harbor ports bustling with world trade and marine products.

In the process of moving downhill, river waters offer some of their greatest wealth. The Columbia River has thirty federal dams and dozens of non-federal projects along its drainage, eleven in Washington alone. These colossal structures represent the spirit of hard work and resourcefulness that can turn a great force into an ally. That's what Woodie Guthrie was singing about.

Backroads along the Columbia River bring forth samples of its diverse personalities. In north-central Washington, the routes pass through river towns that look the same as they did during the 1880s. The sparkling lakes created by all those dams allow for recreation opportunities unimagined by those who constructed the projects. Byways here celebrate the birth of wine appellations and the quirky dreams of millionaires. They mark the place where a river and a mountain range meet—and the river prevails. They pass ports where ships from the world's docks transfer their

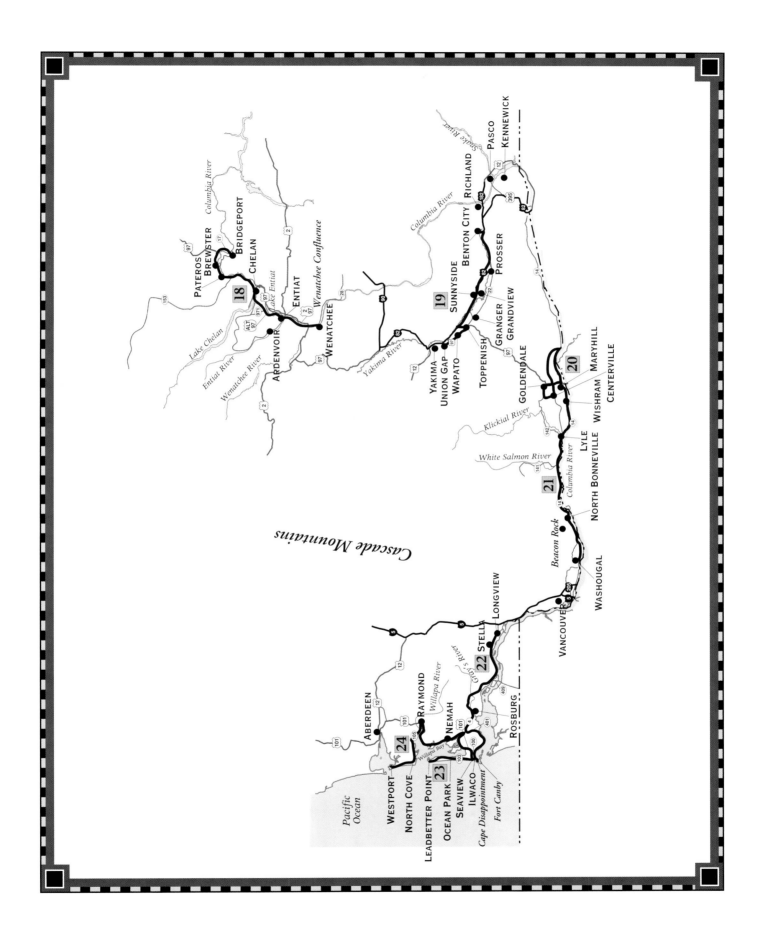

ABOVE:

The face of Chief Joseph Dam has gothic rhythm on a massive scale. This dam supplies power for residents throughout the state through the Bonneville Power Administration.

RIGHT:

A retired turbine blade assembly becomes an elegant modern sculpture in the interpretive park above Wells Dam.

Water from the Columbia River Reclamation Project makes the fertile soil in the state's central plateau productive. Fruit trees (these are apple blossoms) thrive in the region's plentiful sunshine and irrigation.

cargo to trains, trucks, grain elevators, refineries, cold storage plants, and warehouses.

Finally, Columbia River roads embrace the wild coast that hid the mouth of the river so well and today provides prolific habitat for birds, trees, marine life, and people. It's hardly surprising that the proposal to accept the State of Washington into the Union was drafted in a town on the Columbia River, or that the name first proposed for the fledgling state was Columbia.

If you pick only one set of backroads from this book to learn about Washington State, pick these river byways. They show the stages where, in so many themes, irresistible forces have met immovable objects, yielding energy and creativity.

How can travelers take best advantage of this feast of a river? First, remember that an entire state lives downstream and take care not to pollute the waterway. Second, wear a life vest when playing on the Columbia's waters (it's the law) and respect protected habitats and game regulations.

And plan to have fun! As with every other region in Washington, the resources of this mighty river have contributed to a recreation boom. Washington state parks along its waters are crowded with families escaping their daily routine and looking for sunshine. Most commonly seen accessories on the Columbia River byways: fishing boats, speedboats, houseboats, camping gear, binoculars, fishing poles, corkscrews, cameras and easels, oyster knives, kites, those life vests, and sunglasses. Most commonly seen expressions: carefree grins, thoughtful astonishment, and contented sighs.

COLUMBIA RIVER
The Wenatchee River Confluence to Bridgeport

ROUTE 18

From the Wenatchee River Confluence, follow U.S. Highway 97 North through Entiat. There are two routes to Chelan: the first option is to turn left on Washington Highway 971; the second is to stay on Alternate U.S. Highway 97. After Chelan, the alternate highway joins back with U.S. 97. Follow it north through Pateros and Brewster. Turn onto Washington Highway 17 and head west to Bridgeport.

One of the unanticipated outcomes of the September 11, 2001, attack on the World Trade Center in New York City is heightened concern for dam security on the Columbia River. This byway was impacted by changes in tourism policies at hydroelectric dams; now it's lighter on dam tours and heavier on having fun with water.

Start at Confluence State Park where the Wenatchee River meets the Columbia River. Camp, swim, and enjoy this green oasis. Then head east on U.S. Highway 97 and look for the interchange for Alternate U.S. Highway 97 going north, with signs for Rocky Reach Dam and the town of Entiat. Drivers who find themselves on the Odabashian Bridge crossing the Columbia must turn around and come back to the cloverleaf!

As you continue along Alt. U.S. 97, find the exit for Rocky Reach Dam. As of this printing, the dam is open for tours, which include the powerhouse, indoor fish ladder, and interpretive history galleries. As well, the dam complex offers a café, picnic grounds, and a playground. Recently, the turbines in the powerhouse have undergone extensive work, and while they aren't in operation, visitors are allowed to view the workers repairing the turbine equipment and see the differences of scale between humans and these huge structures. None of the three other dams on this backroad provide such access or information on hydroelectric power projects. However, be prepared for an airport-style security check when entering the facility.

From Rocky Beach, continue north on Alt. U.S. 97 as it follows the Columbia River reservoir to Entiat. Actually, this town should be called Entiat III. The first incarnation burned down, and the second was flooded when Rocky Beach Dam was completed and Lake Entiat began to rise. At Entiat, the exit to Ardenvoir also leads to nearly a dozen campgrounds in the Wenatchee National Forest. The U.S. Forest Service ranger station in town dispenses information about the facilities and the forest.

Washington 971 and Alt. U.S. 97 follow the edge of the lake to the recreation boomtown of Chelan on Lake Chelan. This cold, deep mountain lake pushes into the Okanogan National Forest, Wenatchee National Forest, and the North Cascades National Park. Resorts, recreation services, and transportation options are in town, which is sited at the head of the lake near another small dam. There's also a ranger station in Chelan and a wildlife area near the river.

Alt. U.S. 97 rejoins U.S. 97, which crosses the Columbia here. This byway turns left (north) to continue on to the Wells Dam exit. Named after A. Z. Wells, a prominent local orchardist, the earthen dam features huge experimental fish-rearing ponds. A viewpoint above the dam provides interpretive information, splendid views of Lake Pateros, and a huge turbine core with blades.

When you reach the town of Pateros, if you want to return to the west side of the state, look for signs to Alta Lake State Park and Washington Highway 153 connecting to the North Cascades Highway via the scenic Methow Valley. Travelers staying on the current backroad route should continue northeast on U.S. 97 to Lake Pateros and Brewster. Here the lake widens as it merges with the Okanogan River. A bridge at Brewster and good roads around the lake allow this part of the trip to be taken as a loop.

On the north side of the lake, U.S. 97 crosses the Okanogan River and continues north to the town of Okanogan. This route, however, continues east around the lake on Washington Highway 17. Look for signs to visit old Fort Okanogan (once a Hudson Bay Company outpost) after crossing the river. As you near Bridgeport, watch for access to Bridgeport State Park near Chief Joseph Dam.

The legendary leader of the Nez Perce tribe, Chief Joseph spearheaded a masterful retreat from General William T. Sherman's large and fully equipped cavalry across Washington, Idaho, and Montana. The chief posed for Edward Curtis, in 1903, in full ceremonial attire.

RIGHT:

One of the pleasures of touring wine country is learning how different vintners concoct their wines. This winery prefers an oak finish for its products.

BELOW:

Hyatt Vineyards announces its location with a barrel wagon. Wineries located throughout Yakima Valley provide ambience and information in their tasting rooms and patios.

Vineyards roll down a sunny hillside toward the Yakima River. The far side of the river banks against the Horse Heaven Hills.

Yakima Valley's warm days, cool nights, and relatively mild winters have proven to be a productive combination for vineyards.

Chief Joseph was a Nez Perce leader credited with leading his entire tribe in a successful fourteen-hundred–mile military retreat from General William T. Sherman's large, well-provisioned cavalry. This dam, built by the Army Corp of Engineers in 1949 and the second-most productive on the Columbia River, is a worthy legacy, if majestic strength is any criteria. Unlike the three other dams on this byway, Chief Joseph does not serve its county public utility district, but rather the city of Seattle.

The process of building it was another chapter in the boom and bust history of the town of Bridgeport. This little town exploded into being with a gold rush in the 1880s, when it was called Westfield. In 1889, businessman J. Covert of Bridgeport, Connecticut, purchased the town for sixty thousand dollars and renamed it. It was incorporated in 1910 and saw a long bust period in the Depression years. Construction of Chief Joseph Dam turned the lights back on for this tough community, which now serves dam management, agriculture, and the booming recreation industry.

ROUTE 19

This region's wineries are served by Interstate 82, which is bounded at the south end by the Tri-Cities and at the north end by Wapato. To reach the first round of wineries, take the Benton City exit and look for De Moss Road and Sunset Road. Back on Interstate 82, drive northwest; take the Prosser exit to access U.S. Highway 12, also called Wine Country Road. It parallels Interstate 82 but at a much slower pace. Follow that road west, passing through Grandview and Sunnyside. In Granger, head east on Washington Highway 223 to return to Interstate 82 and the wineries in the west valley. At the end of the day, head south on Washington Highway 22 to reach Toppenish and take U.S. Highway 97 northwest to Wapato and Union Gap.

WINE COUNTRY
Yakima Valley from Benton City to Union Gap

The Yakima Valley was born of volcanic soil and water from the Cascade Mountains. The fields in the valley thrive on water drawn from the river by the Rosa and Sunnyside Canals. The sun shines an average of 17.4 hours per day. Growing season days are warm and nights are cool. The winters are mild enough to spare growing grapevines. The soil is rich with volcanic nutrients. This region is the equal of any wine country in the world and, in fact, shares the same latitude as the most famous French wine-producing regions. This valley, the state's first American Viticultural Area (AVA), includes ten thousand acres of grapes and about forty wineries. Like wine tours in other great regions, this byway is not so much a straight journey as instructions for wandering.

Begin by leaving the Tri-Cities (Pasco, Kennewick, and Richland), driving northwest on Interstate 82. Just after leaving Richland, the Yakima River makes a loop, creating an area with a microclimate different from that of the greater Yakima Valley. This area was designated as the Red Mountain AVA in 2001. A dozen wineries have planted just over four thousand acres of Chardonnay, Cabernet Sauvignon, Merlot, and Syrah grapes here. To reach these wineries, take the Benton City exit (exit 95) and look for De Moss Road and Sunset Road.

Return to Interstate 82 and drive northwest to Prosser (exit 82) to access the lower Yakima Valley. The Yakima Valley Highway (U.S. Highway 12), which was the main thoroughfare before the interstate was complete, has now been renamed Wine Country Road. This is a better route for seeking wineries than staying on Interstate 82. The lower valley has nearly a dozen wineries, big and small, located on both sides of the river. And size does matter in regard to wine production. Pick a large and a small winery for comparisons. Learn about differences in equipment, production processes, and taste. Prosser also produces hops, cattle, and tree fruit. Experienced wine country tourists bring coolers to store wine and other foodstuffs purchases during the day. And they pick up a copy of the Yakima Valley Farm Products Guide to complement their wine maps.

Drive west on Wine Country Road until it meets up with Washington Highway 223. In this stretch from Prosser to Granger via Sunnyside and Grandview, the wineries are fewer than in the upper and lower valley. The valley produces red and white wines, with the former slightly predominating, and sells grapes to wineries across the country. Try a couple of varietals that are new to you. Sunnyside has a cheese factory and Grandview has a microbrewery that showcases local hops.

The western part of the Yakima Valley is rich with recreational activities as well as wineries. Consider taking Washington Highway 22 across the Yakima River to Toppenish, where every building of any size sports a historical mural. This town also hosts the cultural center for the Yakima Tribe and full recreational services. Fishing and rafting on the Yakima River are popular.

Photographer Arthur Rothstein, working for the Farm Security Administration, helped document the dignity of farmers struggling through the Depression. This picture, taken in 1936, shows a Yakima Valley worker tying hop vines to overhead wires. This practice allowed for the best development of the flowers that supply pollen to flavor beer. (Courtesy of the Library of Congress)

Mount Adams rules over a valley of wheat just beginning to turn golden.

RIGHT:

Good dreams find a noble death near Chamberlain-Goodnoe Road. Farm consolidation has improved chances of breaking even in dry land agriculture.

ABOVE:

Farmers along Hoctor Road use found objects to individualize their gates and driveways.

RIGHT:

Abandoned houses, tree groves, and a good road are all that remain of the town of Sand Springs, vacated in the 1950s.

Return again to Interstate 82, or to Yakima Valley Highway, to visit the wealth of wineries thriving in the west valley. Many are situated high in the hills above the valley. Vineyards lie like patchwork quilts over the hillsides. Tasting rooms and patios at the hillside wineries have magnificent views of the valley and the river. Summer sunsets are events to be celebrated with a long dinner and a glass of wine. This is a good opportunity to consolidate notes on the day's tasting (and tote up purchases).

Those foodies who are going back to the west side of the Cascades after a day in wine country should save the stretch of U.S. Highway 97 to Wapato for last, so they can pick up fresh fruits and vegetables on the way home to their refrigerators. From July through September, every kind of fresh produce can be purchased from the grower. Lateral "A," a farm road north of Wapato, is a virtual grocery store, with endless stands and fields of foods. It also has an amazing view of Mount Adams.

Concentrating on quality rather than quantity, taking appropriate meals, and perhaps designating a non-drinking driver will keep the wine country experience safe and pleasant. The winemakers of the Yakima Valley produce world-class products and are proud to offer information and insights to wine drinkers of all levels of sophistication. They have nurtured renowned grape varieties, thoughtfully crafted wines, and created charming tasting rooms. Wine tourists give as much care to their task of enjoying the process of learning about wine.

WHEAT RANCHING AND OLD FARMS
Goldendale

This byway has great beauty for those who yearn for Midwest country life, if it could always be lived under spectacular mountains or alongside powerful rivers. This region is sort of like Kansas with amazing accessories. If you come to this byway from the west side of the Cascades, plan an overnight stay in Goldendale or The Dalles on the Oregon side of the Columbia River. Both have complete services.

Farmer John J. Golden founded Goldendale in 1872. It sits at the edge of the Simcoe Mountains (two dozen or so ancient cinder cones) along the Little Klickitat River. Check out the parade of beautifully preserved Victorian homes in Goldendale, including the gem that has been adopted as the Presby Museum. The Goldendale Observatory caps a hill above town. It features the nation's largest public telescope—a twenty-four-inch, hand-ground, amateur-built scope available to visitors on clear nights.

Now take a drive in cattle and wheat farm country. The plateau lands of this byway were the home of the Yakima, Wasco, and Klickitat peoples and then of Scandinavians and Finns who came west in wagon trains. Some of the farm buildings they crafted have been abandoned for air-conditioned digs or life nearer neighbors. But the sunburned remains are poignant witnesses to lives of vision and hard work.

ROUTE 20

This figure-eight-shaped route begins and ends in Goldendale. Drive south on U.S. Highway 97, also called Simcoe Highway. Turn left (east) on Hoctor Road. Turn left at former Sand Springs to connect with old Highway 8. At Rock Creek near the Klickitat tribal hall, turn right at the cattle guard. Continue downhill to reach Washington Highway 14 West. In Maryhill, turn right onto U.S. 97 North.

Head back toward Goldendale, but instead of retracing the previous roads, turn left onto Centerville Highway. Turn right onto Linden Road, then left onto Van Hoy Road, and left again in a mile. Then take the next right onto Finn Ridge Road.

To return to Goldendale, turn right onto Washington Highway 142. In Goldendale, turn left on South Columbus, and then right at the highway sign to Yakima. Meet up with U.S. 97 on the east side of Goldendale.

Drive south on U.S. Highway 97, here called Simcoe Highway, then make a left turn on Hoctor Road. There's a sign for the Red Rock Quarry, which yields the red volcanic rock that homeowners like to use on driveways and garden paths. Mosey past the quarry, as well as cows, sheep, llamas, horses, goats, working and abandoned farms, and, in April and May, fields of wildflowers. Fifteen miles from Goldendale, after a baked wooden farmhouse on the left, look to the right to catch watercolor glimpses of the Columbia River Gorge and Oregon beyond. Pavement runs out on Hoctor Road near a small wind-turbine farm. The gravel road begins to descend via benches—terraces of earth formed along the walls of the river gorge. A magnificent ghost farmhouse marks a left turn onto what was once the main street of Sand Springs, a village abandoned in the 1950s. This road connects with old Highway 8. Continue downhill and into a cottonwood wash, where the Klickitats have a tribal hall, and then turn right at a cattle guard at Rock Creek. At the bottom of the canyon is an estuary popular for fishing.

Arthur Rothstein captured this timeless image of hay-gathering activities near Goldendale in 1936. (Courtesy of the Library of Congress)

Connect with Washington Highway 14 and head west. The Columbia Gorge here is dry grassland studded with fortress rocks on cow-trail-terraced hillsides. Up to twenty-one layers of volcanic flows with diverse patterns of hexagonal columns form canyon walls. Mount Hood guards the south side of the river. Note John Day Dam far below the highway. At Maryhill, take a right turn onto U.S. 97. Head north, back up the canyon side toward Goldendale.

Instead of returning on the previous roads, turn off to the left at Centerville Highway. Country roads follow section lines with periodic ninety-degree turns. They may have cattle or slow-moving vehicles. Relax. Gently rolling fields host beautiful barns and houses among small clutches of shade trees. Birds sing their hearts out. Mount Hood and Mount Adams beacon the north and south side of the plateau.

Turn left onto Van Hoy Road and left again in a mile. Turn right onto Finn Ridge Road. Cows and wheat have it lucky here. Watch for a unique round barn to your right.

Turn right onto Washington Highway 142. While rolling east, note how the prairie farmland drops into the Klickitat River Valley and grows a stubble of pine trees. In the distance, forested mountains may have snow into early summer. The road takes a wide turn south before reaching South

Sam Hill built this model of Stonehenge near his Maryhill estate.

Sam Hill modeled his personal castle at Maryhill after European estates. Now it serves as a museum housing his art collection, including exquisite small sculpture studies by Auguste Rodin.

The Columbia River's sunny northern shores have sprouted vineyards and award-winning wineries.

Columbus Street in Goldendale. At Columbus, turn left, then turn right at a highway sign showing the direction to Yakima. Meet up with U.S. 97 to complete this loop to Goldendale at just under seventy miles.

Backroads like these create nostalgia for the country life, even in those who've never actually lived in the country. Quiet pastures festooned with wildflowers, slow empty roads, towns only five minutes wide, and sweet peaceful skies with sparkling mountains on their edges—what's not to like?

STONEHENGE
Maryhill to Washougal

ROUTE 21

From the junction with U.S. Highway 97 in Maryhill, follow the Columbia River west on Washington Highway 14. End at Washougal, just over eighty miles from the starting point.

Maryhill is a town and a museum. Entrepreneur Sam Hill built a concrete castle three miles west of U.S. 97 and a concrete model of Stonehenge overlooking the Columbia River three miles east of U.S. 97. He named the castle site after his daughter Mary. Besides the castle (now a museum) and monument, Sam is remembered here by a town named Maryhill and the Maryhill State Park.

Drive west on Washington Highway 14, starting from the junction with U.S. 97. This backroad skirts the north side of the river, climbing and dropping at benches and tributary rivers. Signs mark the Columbia Gorge National Scenic Area and significant sites from the Lewis and Clark expedition. In the spring, wildflowers cover every suitable surface of the surrounding terrain. The highway has frequent viewpoint turnouts and threads through a dizzying array of recreation sites. It is a surprisingly popular route for bicyclists.

Four miles west of the junction, look below to see the train switching yards of Wishram, which look toy-like from this vantage point. Not far away is a turnout for Celilo Falls with information about the native and modern history of the site. Look for vineyards along the river and consider the temptations of winery tasting rooms.

Celilo Falls was a tribal fishing site before the Columbia was dammed to yield hydroelectric power. This 1930 postcard captures the scale of the original falls.

The Columbia makes a horseshoe turn where Dallesport is located. The Dalles Dam and a bridge to The Dalles, Oregon, are here, too. Before the river was reined to make hydroelectric power, tribes built wooden platforms for spearing fish at this site. Petroglyphs at Horsethief State Park are further evidence of native handiwork. The park has camping and boat launching facilities.

Windsurfers love the Columbia Gorge and mob to places like Doug's Beach, the Bingen marina, and "the Hatch," a local fish hatchery. Watch them work on days with ideal wind and river conditions.

The Klickitat River enters the Columbia at Lyle. Anglers should stop at any of the three lakes between here and Bingen, a town with many references to its Rhine River counterpart. The White Salmon River also meets the Columbia in this area, and there is a toll bridge to Hood River, Oregon, via Washington Highway 141. Travelers heading west will note that hillside forests grow thicker and grasslands become greener due to increasing precipitation from the Pacific Ocean. Tunnels usher cars through rock outcroppings.

Continuing on Highway 14, Trout Lake and Drano Lake attract boaters and anglers. More recreation sites to check out include the Little White River Recreation Area, Dog Mountain Trailhead, Home Valley, and the Wind River Recreation Area. Look for signs to the Columbia River Interpretive Center and the famous Skamania Lodge. The center offers exhibits and activities to interest families, and a library with resources on the human and natural history of the Columbia Gorge.

The Bridge of the Gods, named for a legendary natural bridge, crosses the Columbia to Cascade Locks, Oregon. Tours of Bonneville Dam are available in the town of North Bonneville. The 848-foot-high volcano plug in Beacon Rock State Park is visible for miles up and down the river. This sentinel marks the beginning of tidal rhythms from the Pacific Ocean and the end of river rapids. Stop for an eyeful of view at Franz Lake Viewpoint.

The St. Cloud Recreation Area is popular for camping and hiking. Another turnout for dazzling views is Cape Horn. Here the river has cut through great walls that are part of the heart of the Cascade Range, and the results are dramatic.

Arrive at Washougal and its twin city, Camas. Huge mills signify the importance of timber cutting and processing to this area. The river valley grows wide and the Columbia River Gorge National Scenic Area ends. But the Columbia still has miles to go.

Lewis and Clark recorded their impressions of this mighty passageway in 1805 and 1806. They would probably not recognize many sections of it now, but modern travelers can still appreciate its dramatic scale and recreation attractions. Mysterious Stonehenge seems to be at home among the Columbia River Gorge's natural and human-made wonders.

LOWER COLUMBIA
Ilwaco to Longview

Ilwaco is a fishing town. Charters and commercial fishermen harbor their boats in a marina that faces a strip of shops. The shops offer bait, bookings, and bibelots, as well as strong hot coffee, net floats, and pictures of prize catches. The heritage museum in town is a good place to start this byway, which showcases the last stretch of a mighty river.

A side trip south, on Washington Highway 100, to Cape Disappointment and its beloved lighthouse brings home some history of this place. John Meares, an explorer and fur trader, named the cape. His great

ROUTE 22

Begin at Ilwaco, at the junction of Washington Highway 100 and U.S. Highway 101. A short drive south on Highway 100 will lead to the dramatic lighthouse at Cape Disappointment. Take U.S. 101 South at Spruce Street, heading for Chinook. Turn onto Washington Highway 401 North at the town of Naselle. Then turn right onto Washington Highway 4 East.

In Rosburg, follow signs to a rare covered bridge. This side route rejoins Highway 4, which passes through Skamokawa and Cathlamet, and ends at Longview.

RIGHT:

Commercial fishing vessels find safe harbor in the Port of Ilwaco.

BELOW:

Cape Disappointment Lighthouse sparkles by day and beacons by night at the mouth of the Columbia River. Its light warns sailors of an area called "the graveyard of the Pacific."

LEFT:

An enterprising raccoon searches a waterway near the Columbia River for a meal.

BELOW:

Near Rosburg, a scenic covered bridge in rural splendor is frequently photographed. It is one of the best covered bridges in the state.

A Tlakluit man nets salmon in this 1910 Edward Curtis photograph. At Wishram, tribal members used natural rock weirs to channel fish, which could be netted from wooden platforms. Migrating salmon provided a major source of food and figured large in legends.

disappointment was that this prominence failed to become the gateway to an inland water passage. (The mouth of the Columbia River was actually discovered by Captain Robert Gray's expedition years later.) The lighthouse, first operated in 1856, is the oldest in the state.

Return to Ilwaco and take U.S. Highway 101 South at Spruce Street. Follow the highway to the town of Chinook, which has a hatchery, boat launch, county park, and picnic area. Beyond is Fort Columbia State Park, a camping ground with a storied history. The Chinook Indians camped and fished here long ago. Captain Gray anchored here during his exploration of the coastline. Lewis and Clark also made camp in this area. The fort shoulders concrete gun emplacements installed for defense in World War II.

U.S. 101 continues into Oregon via the Astoria Bridge, but this route leaves the river, turning north on Washington Highway 401. A state visitor information center and rest area, a mile from the bridge, has maps and facts. Continue to the little town of Naselle, then turn east onto Washington Highway 4 on its way to the Grays River Valley. The landscape celebrates abundant rain with thick forest and banks of ferns.

The town of Rosburg is represented by a small store. Look for signs indicating a detour from the highway to view a splendid covered bridge in a green farm valley.

Return via Highway 4 to the Columbia River at Skamokawa. Here, Redmen Hall houses the River Life Interpretive Museum, and Vista Park offers reasons to linger.

Just east of Skamokawa, look for signs to the Julia Butler Hansen National Wildlife Refuge. In 1972, this bar on Steamboat Slough (fifty-six thousand acres of it) was set aside to preserve habitat for an ark load of animals, including white-tailed deer, tundra swans, elk, salmon, and raptors. Viewing platforms encourage visitors to be naturalists and photographers.

Highway 4 follows the northern edge of the refuge to arrive in Cathlamet, a town stuck in an earlier time. Films such as *Men of Honor* and *Snow Falling on Cedars* have been made in its streets. The Wahkiakum County Historical Museum serves up the area's past. Travelers on Washington Highway 409 to Oregon will catch the little Puget Island Toll Ferry; you can watch it work from a viewpoint.

County Line Park is a staging area for parasailing enthusiasts. Stop and catch them working the forces of wind and water into personal fun.

Highway 4 comes into the wide valley formed where the Cowlitz and Coweeman Rivers meet the Columbia. It emerges from red rock walls into more gentle slopes, with views of Mount St. Helens to the northeast. On the river, the view includes gliding barges and long railroad trestles.

Travelers can stop by the museum in Stella or continue on to Longview. Lewis and Clark camped here on the banks of the Cowlitz River in 1805.

ABOVE:

Sports fishermen on a charter boat out of Ilwaco try their hand at catching salmon.

RIGHT:

Lewis and Clark met the Pacific Ocean here. An interpretive center at Fort Canby State Park commemorates the famous journey of discovery.

Longview was first called Monticello and is the site where Washington Territory's petition for statehood was composed. Citizens wanted the state christened Columbia, but that designation already enjoyed special status as the name of the nation's capital, the District of Columbia. The Long-Bell Logging Company purchased land here, renamed the town, and in 1923, opened a planned community for fourteen thousand timber workers. Today Longview and its twin, Kelso, are still powered by timber and transportation. Travelers connect with Interstate 5 for destinations north, south, and across the Columbia. All services are available.

The Columbia Drainage, second in volume only to the Missouri/Mississippi in the continental United States, pours more water into the Pacific Ocean than any other river in North or South America. This backroad showcases the river's rush to the sea.

LONG BEACH
Fort Canby to Leadbetter Point

ROUTE 23

From Fort Canby, drive north on Washington Highway 100 to its junction with U.S. Highway 101. Turn left on U.S. 101 North (which is also First Street in Ilwaco).
Next, turn left onto Washington Highway 103 North (also called Pacific Highway). Pass through Seaview and Long Beach. In Ocean Park, stay on Highway 103 as it switches from following the west to the east side of the Long Beach Peninsula; the highway is also called Sandridge Road up here. Pass through Nahcotta and Oysterville. To drive as far as possible into Leadbetter Point, turn left on Oysterville Road and right on Stackpole Road.

Begin this byway at Fort Canby. A lot of recorded history began there, too. The Lewis and Clark Corps of Discovery mapped these grounds in the winter of 1805–1806. The buildings that grace the grounds now were constructed from 1896 to 1902. Gunnery bunkers were constructed for coast defense in World Wars I and II. The newly refurbished interpretive center provides military history as well as displays of Chinook Indian culture.

The park is in a complex of recreation sites that includes campgrounds, access to the North Jetty at the mouth of the Columbia River, a U.S. Coast Guard Station, and—via North Head Road—access to the handsome North Head Lighthouse. Attractions at this state park could easily provide a week's worth of exploration for an active family.

To continue on this byway, drive north on Washington Highway 100 (it makes a loop through the northern part of the park) and arrive at the Port of Ilwaco. Recreation supplies and services are available in this town that lives to fish. In Ilwaco, turn left on First Street (also U.S. Highway 101) and continue north. Where U.S. 101 turns right to continue around the Olympic Peninsula, proceed north on Washington Highway 103. Also called Pacific Highway, Highway 103 passes through Seaview and Long Beach. A Long Beach Peninsula visitor bureau is located at the corner where U.S. 101 turns.

Seaview and Long Beach run together and are dedicated to seaside fun. Some of the entertaining diversions include a kite museum, an elevated boardwalk on the beach, numerous humorous sculptures, and all services needed to enjoy a full schedule of fun and festivals. Twenty-eight miles of sand start at Seaview and continue to the tip of the unique land formation. Public access to the broad, sandy ocean beach is unimpeded on the peninsula. Cars can even drive on large portions of the beach.

At the north end of town, look for cranberry bogs in the center of the peninsula and the Cranberry Museum on Pioneer Road. Further north, Loomis Lake State Park offers fishing and day-use facilities. Klipsan Beach has a beach access road for those ending or starting a drive on the beach.

Ocean Park has an interesting history as a former religious camp. Now it offers beach access and all services to vacationers. To reach Pacific Pines State Park, a day-use site with beach access, drive through Ocean Park on Vernon Avenue and watch for signs. At a stop sign in the middle of town, Highway 103 turns right on Bay Street. For the remainder of the trip, it follows the eastern shore of the peninsula as Sandridge Road.

Nahcotta is the site of the Port of Peninsula and the Willapa Bay Interpretive Center. Oysters are the prime crop here, and a state Department of Natural Resources laboratory serves the industry's research and testing needs. Just down the road at Oysterville, the history of the oyster harvest is treasured. This town was founded in 1854 and became a boomtown of five hundred, based on the stories of shellfish harvests from Willapa Bay. For one entire year, Oysterville was the Pacific County seat, until the official public records were stolen by a raiding party from the nearby town of South Bend. Now it is a charming historic seaside village.

Turn left on Oysterville Road, then right on Stackpole Road to enter Leadbetter Point State Park. The end of Stackpole Road signals time to get out the backpack and field glasses. Hiking trails take birders and photographers out to the end of the point within the Willapa National Wildlife Refuge. This spit and the bay it guards swell with seasonal bird migration. Seals and sea lions lounge on Grassy Island, shielded from tourists by swamps and sloughs. Black bears prowl the meadows and dense forests. Whales swim in the waters off the point. The refuge offers many kinds of habitat and solitude for people and wildlife.

Families from the cities on Puget Sound often take annual vacations on the Long Beach Peninsula and never seem to tire of the activities available there. If the weather is kind, the beaches are irresistible. Beach towns on these roads have learned how to delight and entertain visitors indoors as well as out. In fact, it's hard to have a bad time at the Long Beach Peninsula.

WILLAPA BAY
Westport to Ilwaco

This scenic backroad may not travel the shores of the mighty Columbia, but its seven river drainages earn it a place in the "river" chapter. Comparing river and ocean marine ports and landscapes, this route clings to the coast and Willapa Bay, revealing vignettes of life on the edge of the drainages and the sea. A fishing pole and birding equipment are appropriate accessories.

Start with an ocean port, Westport, at the mouth of Gray's Harbor. This city's heart is a busy marina serving its commercial and charter

ROUTE 24

From Westport, drive south on Washington Highway 105 towards Grayland and North Cove. At Raymond, take U.S. Highway 101 South.

Past Nemah, U.S. 101 junctures with Washington Highway 4, but turn right to stay on U.S. 101. Father south, the highway meets with Alternate U.S. Highway 101, but this backroads route continues straight ahead via Seaview to Ilwaco.

ABOVE:
Migrating sandpipers clutch the shoreline, feeding at a stopover in the Willapa National Wildlife Refuge.

FACING PAGE:
Visitors appreciate the view from North Head Lighthouse.

fishing fleet and pleasure craft. Westhaven State Park, on Half Moon Bay, is popular for surfing, fishing, and beachcombing. Pelicans, cormorants, and seals enjoy this beach, too. The Westport Lighthouse sits on Ocean Avenue in Westport Light Park. Other attractions are the maritime museum, and passenger ferry to Ocean Shores across the mouth of the harbor. The town and dunes are reminiscent of Cape Cod.

Exit Westport on Forrest Street, which becomes Washington Highway 105 south of town. Note signs to Twin Harbors State Park, which is located on two small estuaries in the south harbor. Drive amid sand dunes and windswept groves of evergreens. Find beach access at Grayland, or go to Grayland Beach State Park for camping.

So how did everything get this "Gray" name? Is it a comment on the weather? Actually, Captain Robert Gray was a Revolutionary War veteran and entrepreneurial explorer who discovered and named many features of the Pacific Northwest coastline. Those include Gray's Harbor and the entrance to the Columbia River, which he successfully crossed during his first globe-circling journey in 1787 to 1792. The Kuroshio Current, a warm current flowing from Japan, frequently brings clouds to this coastline, but modern visitors explore it in spite of occasional gray skies.

Continue south on Highway 105. Keep going straight to explore the wildlife refuge at Cape Shoalwater, or make a pronounced turn left at North Cove. After the turn, follow signs to historic Tokeland to see the remains of early sea town life. Between North Cove and Raymond, the road crosses the North River and curves along the Willapa River. Raymond is the site of the Port of Willapa, a shipping port for forest products and raw timber. Cross the Willapa River and turn right on U.S. 101 heading south. There's a visitor information center, seaport museum, salmon fishing, and services for vacationers.

South Bend, a few miles away, is a town devoted to oysters. It hosts a Pacific County museum, courthouse, cannery, and a public picnic/fishing pier.

Consider a detour off U.S. 101 to Bay Center, another tiny historic town. At Nemah, the highway leaves the bayside and crosses numerous creeks along the edge of the Willapa Hills. Alongside the Naselle River, look for U.S. 101 to make a right turn towards Ilwaco. Those who miss the turn will find themselves heading unexpectedly east.

Now watch for signs for the headquarters of the Willapa National Wildlife Refuge. The refuge headquarters, complete with interpretative services, are just off U.S. 101. The refuge, established in 1937, together with the adjacent Lewis, Reikkola, and Leadbetter Units, host 250 bird species, 53 mammals, 19 reptiles, fish, and an invasion of Atlantic cordgrass. In migration seasons, this place gives sanctuary to the largest bird populations on the Pacific Coast, as well as a contingent of humans who come to watch them. Birds rest, nest, feed, and rear their young in habitat that also supports bear, deer, elk, bats, and bobcats.

SALMON LIMIT · WESTPORT · WN Wash.

From the refuge, push out to Long Island State Park for camping, hiking, and more birding.

U.S. 101 swings west toward Seaview, where it makes a left turn onto Pacific Highway. Seaview and its close neighbor, Long Beach, offer all recreation needs and services. Continue south to the Columbia River fishing town of Ilwaco.

When Captain Gray figured out how to navigate the tricky bar currents at the mouth of the Columbia River, he named the waters after his ship, the *Columbia Rediviva*. He called the prominence that protects Ilwaco's harbor Cape Hancock. Today it bears the name given by an earlier explorer who wasn't able to confirm the river's existence: Cape Disappointment. Modern travelers are not disappointed by their discoveries on this scenic byway. The route provides unique encounters with wild river and seacoast habitats, as well as appreciation for the economic impact of timber, seafood harvest, and vacation fun.

Salmon fishermen pose for a "bragging rights" photo with their fine catch from a 1955 charter trip out of Westport.

PART V

BEAUTIFUL BREADBASKET

FACING PAGE:

Checkerboards of green and gold spread out below the summit of Steptoe Butte. In excellent weather, the view from the top surveys hundreds of miles.

ABOVE:

Ripening wheat heads dance in spring winds and early afternoon sunlight.

The backroads in this region offer drama and variety. One route winds through deep forests and snow-capped mountains. Another follows a challenging grade into a serpentine river valley. One stretches between a fantasy waterfall and an Old West town. One follows a mighty river at its recreational best. And one climbs a hill that looks like a Babylon Tower to look over a checkerboard kingdom.

These roads are all part of a region of Washington State that feels the rain shadow effect of the Cascade Mountain Range. Forests and farms line these byways, surviving hot summer sun and hard cold winters. Rain is an uncommon event. Fire is both friend and foe. All things that survive in this region are tough.

Visitors come to appreciate the strength and uncommon beauty of this place, which represents a complete escape from urban "sophistication" and brings private encounters with nature and big sky. The dry lands will remind some of the Midwest, with wheat fields to the horizons and weathered farm buildings. The communities are like the towns of innocence, with friendly people, old-fashioned architecture, and history to match. Some visitors will be delighted to careen along dazzling road-building feats for the thrill of the ride. And all of this is to be enjoyed in bright sunshine, in any season of the year.

There are distinctions within this region's backroads, to be sure. In the northern part, the landscape is that of the rugged Selkirk Mountains. These are, in fact, foothills of the Rocky Mountains. All roads are hard-earned passages through these crests. One byway follows Washington's artery, the Columbia River, out of the Selkirks and onto the central plateau lands. The abundance of precious water in this dry, hot place makes the route a recreational gem.

In the southernmost part of this region, another backroad winds through mountainous lands, this time the Blue Mountains. Here, rivers have worked hard to gnaw deep canyons, running at whitewater speed through them. Yet working north just a little, sightseers find rolling wheat land with water conspicuous for its rarity and careful stewardship. Even here, rock and water have crossed to provide some stunning surprises.

In the center of the dry lands is a natural tower, which humans, ancient and modern, are compelled to climb. Seeing across the plateau below for hundreds of miles is always worth the trip. And the trip is through farmlands with working and abandoned machinery and buildings, for added interest.

Vacationers from Puget Sound or Spokane should plan leisurely traveling on these backroads. Call ahead and get overnight accommodations, especially if starting from the west side of the state.

Then take time for frequent stops—for a glass of lemonade at a diner, a picnic at a riverside park, a pullover at the top of a hill to gaze at the view and hear songbirds in the meadow, a reading of history while looking at the place where it was made, an afternoon with a river and a fishing

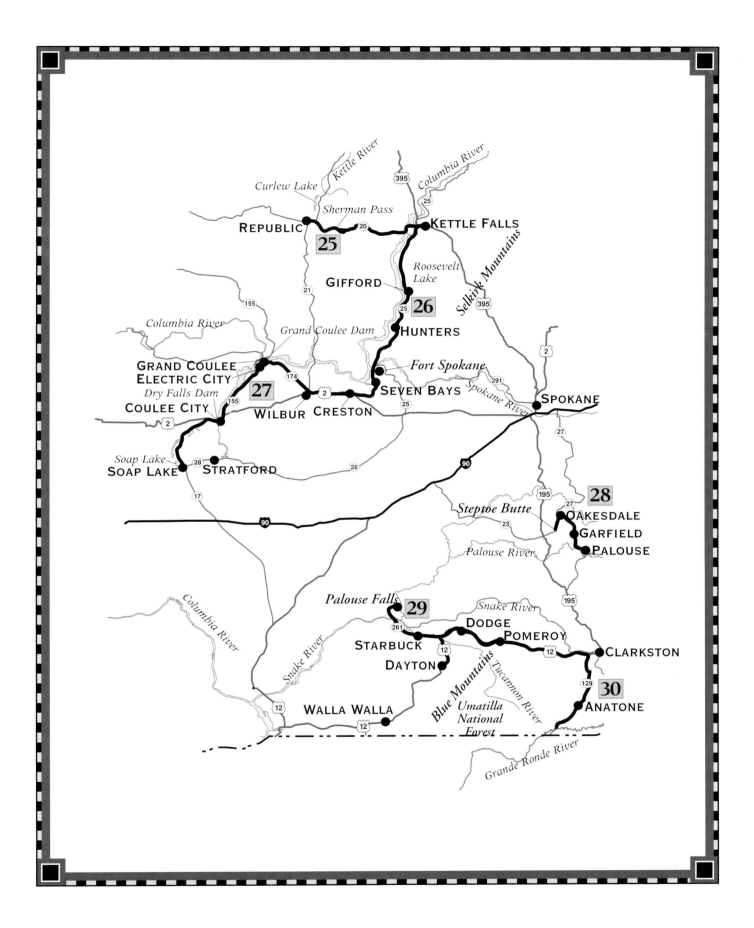

RIGHT:

Sherman Creek carved the canyon used by Sherman Pass Highway to reach the 5,575-foot summit.

BELOW:

Sherman Pass offers motorists a view of the unspoiled Colville National Forest.

Sherman Pass Highway slices through deep forests and the rugged Kettle River Mountain Range.

A farmhouse weathers on a grassy hillside just outside of Republic.

pole, a camp fire, a photo session with an old barn. Those are just a few reasons to allow lots of time for these roads. The dry lands do not, generally, yield up their pleasures to travelers in a hurry. Life is not a race with the clock here so much as a race with the seasons. Drive these byways in the spring to see the region at its greenest. (Check weather and road conditions because snow closures are a possibility.) Air conditioning is seldom required to travel in April and May. Wheat is just pushing up strong green shoots, and undergrowth in ponderosa pine forests provides a show of wildflowers. Or go in summer, when the rivers and reservoirs beckon vacationers to mess about with boats, swim, fish, and raft on wild waters. Go in the fall when the harvest is underway (watch for farm vehicles on rural roads) and vibrant colors emerge in forests and along riverbanks. Some hearty travelers even visit this region in winter with snowmobiles and cross-country skis.

The main thing is to go. This region is a neglected gem. Its lack of steady rain makes the effects of water sculpting dramatic. Unlike countryside in the western half of the state, which has its structure camouflaged with plant life, this region has bare-naked hills and rock-rimmed canyons. Its bones are always showing, and lovely bones they are. The quiet, clean air and big, languid sky are inviting. Miles of wheat have a soothing effect. Sunshine is a fact of life. The main thing is to go.

SHERMAN PASS
Kettle Falls to Republic

ROUTE 25

From Kettle Falls, drive west on U.S. Highway 395, taking the bridge across the lake. Turn left onto Washington Highway 20 South; shortly thereafter, the highway turns right, heading west along Sherman Creek. Follow Highway 20 over Sherman Pass and all the way into Republic.

This backroad is so remote that it passes through territory with a grizzly population. It also has underappreciated solitude and recreation opportunities. Driving from Kettle Falls to Republic, without stopping, will take about an hour and a half. But the woods are lovely, dark and deep, and well worth a few stops.

Begin with a stop in Kettle Falls. The Forest Service ranger station can furnish facts and current conditions. The Kettle Falls Interpretive Center tells how this little town evolved from a Hudson Bay Company outpost to a mission to a boomtown. It also moved when Grand Coulee Dam created Lake Roosevelt, which left the town's namesake falls underwater. Drive west on the U.S. Highway 395 bridge across the lake. Look for a left turn onto Washington Highway 20 South just past the bridge. This route is also known as the Sherman Pass National Scenic Byway.

At the junction of U.S. 395 and Highway 20, campers can choose to go north to campgrounds on the upper Kettle River, or south to those on the west side of Lake Roosevelt. But, if you want to keep to this byway, stay on Highway 20 South, bearing west at Sherman Creek, the drainage that serves as the highway's companion into the Colville National Forest.

All along this side of the pass there are enticing turns to recreation opportunities: Trout Lake, Log Flume Heritage Site (with artifacts of early timber-cutting), and the Canyon Creek Campground and Bangs Mountain

Scenic Drive. The road is walled with ponderosa, larch, and Douglas fir forest as it gently climbs alongside Sherman Creek. There's no need to rush. Impeding other cars is unlikely here. It would be a shame to miss slice views or, worse, to hit a deer, elk, mountain goat, or moose.

Highway 20 leaves Sherman Creek, just as the creek turns north, and begins a climb to Sherman Pass. The pass is named for the famous Civil War general, William T. Sherman, who traveled here in the 1860s. Feet blazed the original path that would become this byway. Early peoples used this route to travel south and east for trade, hunting, and fishing. At 5,575 feet, this is the highest maintained pass in the state. At the top of the pass, look for a short trail that offers a clear view of the Kettle River Range. Columbia Mountain, to the north, and Snow Peak, south, predominate, with White Mountain visible in the southern distance. Near the summit is a silver forest. Weathered snags mark the paths of fires that happened in the 1990s; this clearing also provides browse for black-tailed deer and allow for clear views of the wild terrain.

The road descends toward the Sanpoil River, passing the White Mountain Interpretive Center. Here, switchbacks in the highway require your complete attention.

Highway 20 curves north to meet the Sanpoil River and connect with Washington Highway 21. If you're an angler, head north on Highway 21 to the state park and excellent fishing at Curlew Lake. Otherwise, at the junction, keep to the left and mosey westward into Republic.

Republic has adopted a weathered western theme for its architecture and entertainment. It didn't have to alter much to arrive at the look. Grub and buggy fuel are available. The town was founded on discoveries of silver and gold. Mining continues there today, though recreation is the new gold in the hills. Snowmobilers use the town as a base camp in winter, as do hikers in summer. A Forest Service ranger station has permits and current trail and backcountry conditions.

Take Klondike Road to Old Cemetery Road to reach the town's cemetery, which is plotted on a hill with a sweet view of the Sanpoil Valley looking eastward.

For something completely different, stop at the Stonerose Fossil Center, located on Kean Street. For a small fee, get a lecture on Republic's geologic history, a couple of simple tools, a stone-splitting demonstration, and the opportunity to touch the ages. Do-it-yourself paleontology is fruitful here because of access to deposits from a fertile Eocene Epoch lakebed. The name Stonerose comes from this site's fossils of the earliest forms of Rosacae plant species. Some rules apply: All finds must be inspected by the staff at the center, which holds the right to retain valuable specimens, and after that, prospectors can take three fossils home. Visitors have unearthed discoveries that traveled to the Smithsonian Institution to complete fossil collections there.

Sherman Pass is the kind of backroad that may not appeal to all travelers; its remote and un-enhanced charm requires some effort to

Reviled by some, revered by others, General William T. Sherman led the Union army to victory during the Civil War, then went on to stamp out Indian resistance in the Pacific Northwest during the building of the transcontinental railroad.

Roosevelt Lake, the reservoir created by Grand Coulee Dam, offers camping, fishing, boating, and other recreation opportunities.

RIGHT:

Small car ferries carry riders across Roosevelt Lake to the Colville Indian Reservation lands on the west side.

BELOW:

Electric City houses technicians and service workers for the Grand Coulee Dam hydroelectric project.

appreciate. But for those who want to experience nature without limits, this is a deeply satisfying passageway.

LAKE ROOSEVELT
Grand Coulee Dam to Kettle Falls

ROUTE 26

From Grand Coulee Dam, drive south on Washington Highway 155 to the junction with Washington Highway 174, then head southeast on Highway 174. In Wilbur, connect with U.S. Highway 2 going east to Creston. Just past Creston, turn left off U.S. 2, following signs north and east to Hawk Creek, Seven Bays, and Fort Spokane. Connect with Washington Highway 25 at the site of Fort Spokane. Follow Highway 25 north through Enterprise, Fruitland, Hunters, Cedonia, Gifford, Daisy, and Rice, ending at Kettle Falls.

Woody Guthrie wrote the enthusiastic song "Roll on Columbia" about the colossal Grand Coulee Dam construction project. The statistics on this project are impressive: It is made of 12 million cubic yards of concrete, is 550 feet high and 500 feet wide at the base, and it holds back a reservoir 151 miles long. It was built during the Depression years of 1933 to 1942 by workers laboring in round-the-clock shifts. The dam is now the site of a laser light show on summer nights. It's also the beginning of a string of recreational opportunities that extends to Kettle Falls, all encompassed in the Lake Roosevelt National Recreation Area.

These backroads traverse a feast of thirty-five campgrounds (twenty-eight are National Park Service facilities) on 660 miles of shoreline. Stop by the National Recreation Area headquarters in the town of Grand Coulee for information on camping and fishing.

Heading out of Grand Coulee, drive south to the junction of Washington Highways 155 and 174. Following Highway 174 southeast, drive twenty remarkably straight miles to Wilbur. Just before Highway 174 connects with U.S. Highway 2 at Wilbur, look for a left-turn exit to Washington Highway 21, which leads to camping and boat launch facilities at Penix Canyon.

Back on Highway 174, arrive at Wilbur and head east on U.S. 2 to Creston with its wheat-land railroad connections. Just east of this townlet, look for the turn off to Hawk Creek, Seven Bays, and Fort Spokane. This road works downhill to Hawk Creek, and from here on, drivers are usually within sight of the lake. The broad confluence of the Columbia and Spokane Rivers beneath Johnny George Mountain was, historically, a fishing site for area tribes. In 1880, settlers established Fort Spokane, which became an Indian boarding school after 1898. An interpretive center and walk-around help visitors envision life in this military outpost. Camping, boating, and fishing are still popular in the area. Leaving Fort Spokane on Washington Highway 25, cross the Spokane River, and enter the Spokane Indian Reservation.

Grand Coulee Dam was and is a tourist attraction of large scale. This 1940s postcard shows visitors touring the colossal dam by trolley.

Grand Coulee Dam was were constructed to give the region irrigation, electricity, and flood control, but the resulting lake brings sparkling blue grace to the valley between Rainy Ridge and the Huckleberry Range. Enterprise and Fruitland are tiny ghost farm villages. Find a store and gas at Hunters. The town of Cedonia is located at a crossroads near Harvey Creek. At Gifford, find a free car ferry and three campgrounds. There's a boat launch at Daisy and, after passing the town of Rice on Cheweka Creek, another at Bradbury Beach.

The stretch from Fort Spokane to Kettle Falls is a beautiful, easy drive, but it's just as popular to travel here by boat. Most of those who boat this passage bring their fishing gear. Walleye, trout, perch, burbot, Kokanee salmon, and white sturgeon challenge anglers who prefer to troll under shoreline cliffs or where creeks and rivers come together. Stores and cafés along this backroad sport snapshots of prize catches, and it's easy to strike up a conversation about baits and lures.

One hundred ten miles from Grand Coulee Dam, Kettle Falls has full services and more nearby campgrounds and boat launches. An information center has excellent ideas for those going further on the Columbia River. Near the bridge at Kettle Falls is the site of Saint Paul's Mission and the Mission Point Trail. The Kettle Falls Historical Center is adjacent. Mission Point overlooks the old Fort Colville site, now underwater as part of Lake Roosevelt. The falls was one of the most popular fishing sites for area tribes when David Thompson first arrived here in 1811 on behalf of the Northwest Company. This town is the gateway to the Sherman Pass National Scenic Byway and the last place to fill the gas tank before arriving at Republic forty miles later.

When Grand Coulee Dam was completed and Lake Roosevelt was rising behind the proud engineering feat, very few residents, let alone government planners, could envision the changes coming to the Columbia River. The Lake Roosevelt National Recreation Area evolved as the waters rose. It was a good pairing; natural and cultural resources and popular recreation sites have been developed and protected. The scenic canyon that held the once-wild river is now home to a beloved lake that begs to be enjoyed. Drive it on a summer weekend, with a boat in tow.

The Spokane tribe occupied the valley that still bears its name. Here, tribal members visit photographer Edward Curtis at his campsite in 1910. (Courtesy of the Library of Congress)

Dry Falls
Soap Lake to Grand Coulee Dam

Summer Falls on Billy Clapp Lake is just off Washington Highway 28 near Stratford. It could be considered an appetizer for the Dry Falls byway. It's about ten miles east of Soap Lake, and gives a taste of the geology that created the scenery on this tour.

The Missoula Floods, which shaped this canyon twelve thousand years ago, were epic. They swept all the topsoil and forests from half of the region that is eastern Washington into Oregon's Willamette River Valley and the Pacific Ocean. And these catastrophes happened as many as forty times during the retreat of the most recent ice age.

ROUTE 27

From Soap Lake, drive north on Washington Highway 17. Take the Park Lake Road exit to Sun Lakes–Dry Falls State Park. Back on Highway 17, drive north to Dry Falls Dam and turn right on U.S. Highway 2, heading east. In Coulee City, take Washington Highway 155 north to Electric City and Grand Coulee Dam.

*Picnicking, fishing, and hiking,
with views of Summer Falls on
Billy Clapp Lake, are some of
summer's pleasures.*

RIGHT:

*The "soap" in Soap Lake is a
combination of seventeen minerals
that leach into the water from
surrounding rock. Wind whips up
suds, which line the shores.*

*This sagebrush mariposa tulip lily (*Calochortus macrocarpus*) blooms on the hillsides above Lake Lenore in late spring.*

A vintage sign signals hospitality in the scrublands near Banks Lake.

Plateau lands east of Lower Grand Coulee produce bumper crops of wheat.

Soap Lake is part of a chain of lakes lying in an ancient channel carved by the Columbia River during the floods. The "soap" in the lake is a unique cocktail of minerals that leech into the water from its bedrock. No fish can live in the mix, but humans, from ancient to modern times, have exploited the water's healing properties. Washington Highway 17 passes the southeast end of the lake at the town of Soap Lake, and this byway starts at the visitor center in Lakeview Park. Drive north on Highway 17 into geologic history. The basalt rock walls that cradle these lakes are vast in scale. Layers of lava flows created the pillars that yielded here to the Missoula Floods. Get out of the car and see them up close. Lake Lenore is next in the chain. Look for signs to the Lenore Caves, convenient shelter and storage for ancient peoples, with great views of the canyon.

Steamboat Rock stands as an impressive survivor of the scouring Missoula Floods. This 1940s postcard reveals the remnants of an old fort in the grasslands south of the behemoth rock.

Alkali Lake is next. Its toxic properties were probably well known to cow punchers who herded their commodities from Oregon to the Caribou and Thompson valley pastures in the 1800s. A Caribou Cattle Trail marker tells their story. Blue Lake is next in the chain and a favorite with anglers. Just past Blue Lake, look for the Park Lake Road exit. This leads around Park Lake to the Sun Lakes–Dry Falls State Park, a 4,027-acre site with all amenities including a golf course, store, and restaurant on the western shore. Look up to see the Dry Falls Visitor Interpretive Center four hundred feet above on the canyon wall. Another three miles beyond Sun Lakes is the Deep Lake campground and picnic area.

Return to Highway 17 and look for the exit to that interpretive center. Take the opportunity to visualize how this venerable rock wall was hewn by plunging floodwaters twelve thousand years ago. Get answers to questions about plants and animals seen along the byway.

At Dry Falls Dam, turn right and cross the bridge to Coulee City on U.S. Highway 2 East. This town was a stop on the Caribou Cattle Trail and still stops motorists with an inviting municipal park. In Coulee City, look for signs to Washington Highway 155 North and follow it around the eastern shore of Banks Lake. This thirty-one-mile reservoir, created by Dry Falls Dam in the 1950s, supplies water to the farm fields of the Columbia Basin, as well as Summer Falls. It also supplies anglers with tournament-caliber walleye and bass. Sheer cliffs of basalt wall the reservoir, holding nests for bald eagles and golden eagles. Cranes, geese, pelicans, and ducks also exploit the reservoir, as do mule deer, bobcats, and coyotes. A Bureau of Reclamation designated area protects their habitat.

Steamboat Rock is visible for miles in this coulee. It is located in a well-provisioned state park that occupies nine hundred acres on a peninsula in Banks Lake. Take a two-mile hike to the top for an eagle's view of the territory. On leaving the park, heading north, look for access to the Devil's Punchbowl. (The devil serves punch?)

Continue on Highway 155 to Electric City. Banks Lake extends right up to "the eighth wonder of the world," Grand Coulee Dam. This concrete dam, wedged in a narrow place in the coulee walls, invites superlatives. It is the largest concrete structure on the planet, and includes enough material to make a sidewalk four feet wide and four inches thick that circles the planet twice. Its construction created jobs and inspired optimism during the Depression years. Now, the dam is a tourist attraction, and the visitor information center hosts sightseers from around the world. Hike up to the Crown Point Overlook or the Candy Point Trail to see the entire dam complex. On summer evenings, watch the nightly laser light show on the dam's face. Look for huge siphon tubes next to the dam that keep Banks Lake topped up.

Electric City and its twin across the river, Coulee Dam, have all services. In Electric City, look for the enchanting Gerhke Windmills Garden, a testament to personal creativity.

Grand Coulee Dam, for all its impressive size and strength, would not survive the Missoula Floods. It sits in bedrock cut by the rushing waters. This byway is chockablock with humbling reminders of the power of those floodwaters.

STEPTOE
Palouse to Steptoe Butte

The little town of Palouse may soon find itself on a newly designated Washington State Scenic Byway. Seems travelers from Spokane and even the Puget Sound cities have warmed to the sweet rural delights of this wheat-growing region. Although Steptoe Butte is the significant destination for this byway, weathered barns, antique farm equipment, and farmhouses nestled in groves of trees along the route inspire photographs and nostalgia.

Palouse sits on the river of the same name in a region that was populated by the Palouse tribe. They were noted for their horsemanship and a unique breed of horses with dappled fur. The breed is now called Appaloosa, a contraction of "a Palouse's" horse.

Drive north from Palouse on Washington Highway 27 through endless rolling hills planted with wheat or pasturing beef cattle. Photographers seek vignettes of weathered farm life here like miners pan for gold. Courteous visitors observe some rules: First, ask for permission to enter private lands; second, leave everything exactly as it was, including pasture gates; and third, be sensitive to fire danger in dry grasslands.

The highway passes Garfield, which has a population of 544, a quiet city park, and beautiful old homes. Next is Belmont, which consists of a grain elevator. Oakesdale is twenty-two miles from Palouse, but these are country miles, made to be taken slowly and without cellular phones. Oakesdale has a population of 346 with some of its citizens residing in homes on the National Historic Register. Pick up bottled water or other beverages here.

ROUTE 28

From Palouse, drive north on Washington Highway 27, passing through Garfield, Belmont, and Oakesdale. In Oakesdale, turn left onto Hume Road, following signs to Steptoe Butte State Park. At the park entrance, turn right and follow the road to the summit of the butte.

FACING PAGE, TOP:
Freshly baled hay soaks up a little more summer sun on a hillside near Farmington.

FACING PAGE, BOTTOM LEFT:
Irrigation via the Columbia River Reclamation Project made the arid plateaus of eastern Washington burst with agricultural possibilities.

FACING PAGE, BOTTOM RIGHT:
Harvest crews move quickly to cut and thresh wheat.

ABOVE:
Wheat turns to gold under the summer sun.

Wheat grows in abundance on eastern Washington's rolling, sunny hills. In 1915, it was harvested with steam machines, horse power, and human sweat. Asahel Curtis made this record of the work. (Courtesy of the Washington State Historical Society)

Turn left onto Hume Road, following signs to the state park. It's almost eight miles from the turn to the butte itself, and this country road continues in dry land farm territory. All the while, the butte gets closer and bigger.

Geologically, Steptoe Butte is a formation of pink quartzite. It is a remnant of shoreline from the young North American continent, pushed inland and surrounded by a plateau of lava flows, which were scoured to their basalt core by epochal flooding at the end of the last ice age. Historically, it's a prominent landmark believed to facilitate vision quests by tribes of the region. Later, it was the site of military reconnaissance and, even later, a grand hotel built by an eccentric entrepreneur. Now, it's the apex of a 150-acre state park with a view unequaled.

At the entrance to the park, turn right to begin the spiral up the butte. Though it's less than four miles from the turnoff to the summit, this part of the drive seems to take a long time. Maybe that's because there is so much to look at on the way up. Stands of ponderosa pine, Douglas fir, and apple trees near the base give way to open grassy hillsides towards the top. The park harbors deer, elk, coyote, and rabbits. Hawks use the upper reaches of the butte for launching food searches, while pheasant and quail seek the grasslands and tree cover.

At the top, very few amenities impede the view. With good weather, it is possible to see the Cascade Mountains over 120 miles to the west, as well as the Blue Mountains to the south. The farmland at the base of the butte is laid out in squares with roads binding them together. Park in an ample lot and take a short walk to picnic tables and barbeques. Toilets are available, but water is not. Some motorists bring bicycles and coast back down the hill.

Geologists now speak of structures like this one as a "steptoe" formation, but the butte was named for Colonel Edward Steptoe, a cavalry commander charged with keeping peace in times when tribes were being forced to move to reservations. He used the butte to scout the movements of the Spokane and Nez Perce tribes and locate new farms and settlements. His career is remembered for a failed attempt to force Spokane Indians to leave settlement lands near Rosalia.

Local tribes called the butte "Eomoshtoss" or Power Mountain. They went to the mountain on personal vision quests to seek their totems and strengths.

The colorful "Cash-Up" Davis is another visionary in the butte's recorded history. He built a bustling business with a hotel on his homestead below and dreamed of multiplying his fortune by opening a luxury inn on top of the butte—an inn boasting modern amenities and even an observatory with a telescope. He built his dream hotel in 1888, and it did generate a lot of business at first. But after people had been up to see the place, they didn't come back for repeat visits. The hotel was little used when it burned down in 1908.

Steptoe Butte has hosted a lot of dreams. Maybe dreaming is easier with vistas so vast.

PALOUSE FALLS
Palouse Falls to Pomeroy

In the middle of hot, sagebrush hillsides, the awe-inspiring plunge of Palouse Falls is a magnificent surprise. It's not hard to believe that ancient peoples considered this a sacred place. The state park has numerous footpaths allowing visitors to get up close and appreciate the cathedral-like atmosphere created by the falls and surrounding cliffs.

The park is about three miles off Washington Highway 261. This is the starting place for a journey that salutes the farmers who grow wheat for the world. From the park entrance, drive east on Highway 261 and find the signs for Lyon's Ferry State Park. This location, at the confluence of the Palouse and Snake Rivers, is where pioneers made passage across the water to homesteads in central Washington and other parts of the Pacific Northwest. Now a modern highway bridge and a striking railroad bridge cross the Snake here, and the state park is a water recreation paradise.

Highway 261 continues southeast along the Tucannon River until reaching the tiny town of Starbuck, established in 1883. But before arriving at Starbuck, notice signs for a side trip to Little Goose Dam and Lock. This is a mammoth structure on the Snake River, and is currently slated to be breached to in order to preserve native salmon populations. The lock portion of the structure allows grain boats to come down the Snake River from Lower Granite Lake. Little Goose Dam sits about eight miles off the highway in the middle of tawny hills that shimmer in the heat. Excellent fishing attracts anglers from all around.

Back on Highway 261, head southeast to a junction with U.S. Highway 12. The highway follows the river in a valley lined with seas of wheat. In spring, fresh shoots give the hillsides a supernatural green, followed, over early summer, by the golden-colored ripples of ripening grain.

Arrival at the junction brings a decision. A quick poll of waitresses at Pomeroy suggests that, if time is no object, farm fans should turn south on U.S. 12 and then east on Tucannon Road. (Note that this alternate route is not suitable for RVs or vehicles towing trailers.) Tucannon Road follows the river into a gradually narrowing valley that leads, eventually, into the Blue Mountains. This gem of a valley is intimate in scale and green even in summer. A one-room schoolhouse and village church rest silently from their days of work in the village of Tucannon. Just as the road crosses from Columbia into Garfield County, it turns sharply north and climbs

ROUTE 29

From Palouse Falls State Park, drive east on Washington Highway 261, passing through the town of Starbuck. At the junction of Highway 261 and U.S. Highway 12, you have two options. Either turn south on U.S. 12, then turn left on Tucannon Road, then reconnect with U.S. 12 east near Pomeroy, or continue east at the junction on U.S. 12, passing through Dodge on your way to Pomeroy.

RIGHT, TOP:
Palouse Falls crashes into a colossal basalt bowl created by massive glacial run-off at the end of the last ice age.

RIGHT, BOTTOM:
The Garfield County seat in Pomeroy still serves county business matters. It was built in 1901 after an earlier wood-frame structure burned to the ground.

FACING PAGE:
Washington Highway 261, in spring, winds along green creek drainages on the way to Palouse Falls.

A topographical survey—conducted between 1853 and 1855 to determine the best rail route from the Mississippi River to the Pacific Ocean—yielded this lovely image. John Mix Stanley, an artist who traveled with the party, sketched the spectacular falls on the "Peluse" River, which was translated into this hand-colored lithograph and included in the final report to Congress.

out of the valley to rejoin U.S. 12. The twisty gravel road back onto plateau elevations is daunting, but the views of the valley along the way are worth it.

Drivers who want the wheat-lands experience without risking their road machines will continue east on U.S. 12 at the junction. This route follows the Pataha Creek drainage through plateau lands of wheat, wheat, and wheat. It's lovely to think of the good food that begins on this plain. Pataha Creek has historical meaning as the site of a meeting between Lewis and Clark and a chief of the powerful Nez Perce tribe.

From Dodge, U.S. 12 continues east along the creek to Pomeroy. The total length of the byway, for those who stay on U.S. 12, is forty miles. Pomeroy has great charm and history, starting with its turn-of-the-century, brick-and-stone county courthouse, featuring a statue of Justice with her eyes wide open. The town was justly proud of its designation as county seat, having won it by an act of Congress in 1884 from nearby Pataha City. Pomeroy was built for cattlemen, but acquired a mill when wheat farming became predominant. In June, the town celebrates Pioneer Days. There is a ranger station for information and permits pertaining to the nearby Umatilla National Forest and Wenaha Tucannon Wilderness in the Blue Mountains.

Acres of wheat may seem like an unlikely reason to take a road trip. They have a homogenous texture and function that may not seem exciting to some. But those fields bear witness to the character, muscle, and sweat of the people who made a bet with the land and the sky. It's worth going to see how well the bet has paid this season and to know that we are all winners.

BLUE MOUNTAINS
Dayton to the Grand Ronde River

ROUTE 30

From Dayton, drive north and east on U.S. Highway 12, passing through Dodge and Pomeroy. In Clarkston, turn right onto Washington Highway 129 South. In Asotin, turn right to stay on Highway 129. Follow Highway 129 as it snakes down Rattlesnake Grade toward the Grand Ronde River.

Built in 1887, Dayton's city hall was the envy of towns for miles around. Much of this farm hub town remains the same as when the elegant building was constructed. The town's founders saw their fortunes in civic power and a railway connection to serve agriculture. Dayton's railroad depot is the oldest existing one in the state, built in 1881. Today, recreation services, a food processing plant, wineries, and antique stores occupy many citizens of Dayton. Take a picnic to the park alongside the Touchet River.

From Dayton, drive on U.S. 12, which pushes first north and then east to Pomeroy. It curves through smooth canyons and hills settled with picturesque farms, and it sometimes climbs and cruises along flat plateau terrain. (See the Palouse Falls route for an alternate course through the Tucannon River Valley.)

Pomeroy is the next town with full services. It, too, has a historic city hall and county seat building. Tourists hungry for Midwest-type experiences will feel at home in the diners with racks of private coffee mugs for local customers. Like many sites on this byway, Pomeroy was a stopover camp for Lewis and Clark. You can camp here, too. Check in at the National Forest ranger station for permits before venturing into Umatilla National Forest.

Continuing east, the road runs over wheat land; it is moving to see so many amber waves of grain. At Pataha Creek, find another historical marker at the site of a meeting between Lewis and Clark and the chief of the Nez Perce tribe.

U.S. 12 passes Alpowa Summit and then Chief Timothy Park; a green oasis in the brown rock hills, the park offers waterfront activities that are a magnet on hot summer afternoons. Observe wildlife for yourself at the adjacent Chief Timothy Habitat Management Area.

Now the byway features five miles of brake-testing downhill roadway over sagebrush slopes into the Snake River Canyon. This river has carved further into the lava-layered hillsides than the Colorado River has into the Grand Canyon. U.S. 12 was built to get travelers to Clarkston and its companion across the Snake River, Lewiston, Idaho, marking what was the last navigable segment of the river. Now these towns serve the needs of adventurers who enjoy white-water rafting in nearby Hell's Canyon. Stop at the visitor information center at Fifth and Bridge Streets in Clarkston for permits, maps, and travel tips.

In Clarkston, turn right onto Washington Highway 129 South. Follow the Snake River about five miles to the town of Asotin. A historical museum and Chief Looking Glass Park tell the story of this area. Fill up on gasoline in Asotin because it is seventy-seven miles to the next opportunity. Now turn right on Highway 129, heading uphill out of the Snake River Canyon and onto flat farmland again. The highway passes through sun-baked Anatone on its way to Fields Spring Park, perched on the edge of the Grand Ronde River Canyon.

The highlight of this byway is about to begin. Rattlesnake Grade, just beyond Field Springs, is an aptly named road segment that goes from the high flatlands to the Grand Ronde River. It is a sports-car commercial kind of road with astounding views of the Blue Mountains and the river far below. Drivers will need to keep their eyes on the winding road, however, and not look at the view except at designated turnouts. Like many of the best backroads, this roadway is testimony to the engineering craft and persistence of its builders. Perhaps drivers should also get credit for being willing and eager to tackle Rattlesnake Grade.

At the bottom of the hill is beautiful river landscape. Travelers can return north and get a review of the grade going uphill, or head south on Oregon Highway 3.

Farmland touring is an acquired taste for city-dwellers. But it soothes a curiosity and hunger to know where daily bread comes from and who wrings it from the soil and sun. These backroads answer that hunger with reassuring bounty. As a bonus, there are hours of peace and quiet for travelers who take the time to listen.

OVERLEAF:
Rattlesnake Grade descends 2,500 feet from Field Springs State Park to the Grand Ronde River at the edge of Puffer Butte.

INDEX

Hood Canal lies gemlike in this view from a small airplane on an exceptionally clear day.

SUGGESTED READINGS

Alt, David, and Donald Hyndman. *Roadside Geology of Washington*. Missoula, Mont.: Mountain Press Publishing Co., 1984.

Brokenshire, Doug. *Washington State Place Names: From Alki to Yelm*. Caldwell, Idaho: Caxton Press, 1993.

Carpenter, Cecelia S. *They Walked Before: The Indians of Washington State*. Tacoma, Wash.: Tahoma Research, 1989.

Ford, John K. B., Graeme M. Ellis, and Kenneth C. Balcomb. *Killer Whales: The Natural History and Genealogy or Orcinus Orca in British Columbia and Washington State*. Seattle: University of Washington Press, 2000.

Kirk, Ruth, and Camala Alexander. *Exploring Washington's Past: A Road Guide to History*. Seattle: University of Washington Press, 1990.

La Tourrette, Joe. *Washington Wildlife Viewing Guide*. Helena, Mont.: Falcon Publishing Co., 1992.

DeVoto, Bernard A., ed. *The Journals of Lewis and Clark*. Rev. ed. New York: Mariner Books, 1997.

Mueller, Marge, and Ted Mueller. *Washington State Parks: A Complete Recreation Guide*. 2nd ed. Seattle: Mountaineers Books, 1999.

Parker, Tom. *Discovering Washington Wines: An Introduction to One of the Most Exciting Premium Wine Regions*. Seattle: Raconteurs Press, 2002.

Ritter, Harry. *Washington's History: The People, Land and Events of the Far Northwest*. Portland, Ore.: WestWinds Press, 2003.

Sedam, Mike. *Olympic Peninsula: The Grace and Grandeur*. Stillwater, Minn.: Voyageur Press, 2002.

Sedam, Mike. *Our Seattle*. Stillwater, Minn.: Voyageur Press, 1998.

Sheely, Terry W. *Washington State Fishing Guide*. 8th ed. TNS Communications, 2001.

ABOUT THE AUTHOR
AND PHOTOGRAPHER

Dr. Diana Fairbanks teaches painting and drawing at Kirkland Art Center, and she exhibits her artwork throughout the Pacific Northwest. Previously a university instructor and professional writer, she holds a doctorate in Educational Technology from the University of Washington. A lifelong Washington resident, Fairbanks grew up in the Seattle area, taking frequent trips over the Cascade Mountains to visit family in the dry lands. Fairbanks writes that as a child, "I believed, and still do, that writing and painting/drawing are two arms of the same thing: images translated for others to understand." *Backroads of Washington* is her first book.

Mike Sedam has photographed the Washington landscape for over thirty years. Based out of Seattle, he maintains a stock library of over 60,000 images. Working on assignment for the travel industry, Sedam also shoots images throughout the fifty states, as well as Canada, Mexico, the Caribbean, and Europe. His photographs illustrate several books, including *Olympic Peninsula: The Grace and Grandeur* and *Seattle*, both published by Voyageur Press, and *Hawaii*. He lives in Bonney Lake, minutes away from one of his favorite pictorial subjects, Mount Rainier.